THANKS LORD, I NEEDED THAT!

CHOICE BOOKS
THE BEST IN *FAMILY READING*
P. O. Box 706
Goshen, IN 46526
We Welcome Your Response

THANKS LORD, I NEEDED THAT!

by Charlene Potterbaum

LOGOS INTERNATIONAL
Plainfield, New Jersey

the zaniest, funniest family that ever lived. As the "baby of the family" growing up among you, I was continually inspired by the humor that I saw in all of you. Thank you, beloved clan, for teaching me how to laugh at myself, and how to laugh at life:

my deceased father, O.V. Kendall
my mother, Ruby Kendall
my brothers, Roger, Bob, and Allen
but especially, and most gratefully,
my sister, Mrs. Lauraine (Kendall) Holycross
and, of course—and most importantly—my dear
husband, Gene, who has willingly spent so many years
with the by-product of the clan's influence

ACKNOWLEDGMENTS

Thank you, Sue McGee, for having the patience to decipher the first draft of my manuscript and type it so beautifully.

Thank you, Carol Dykstra, for such tender editing.

Thank you, Judy Gilbert, for some finishing touches.

Thank you, precious prayer group, for crying with me.

Thank you, dear children, for keeping me humble.

Thank you, dear saints of God, for allowing your stories to be used.

Thank you, Toni, for your words of encouragement.

Thank You, Lord, for making it all possible.

PREFACE

Readers aren't aware of it, but every book has at least twenty-seven prefaces, and I'd say roughly 203 first paragraphs. But fortunately, you, the reader, are subjected to only one of each. And while I, the frenzied writer, am wondering about both, an efficient and able publisher is doing his best to create a smashing book cover and title for you.

One time my husband, Gene, asked me, "Why bother with a preface? Most people don't even read them." And suddenly I realized that prefaces are for writers!

I looked a bit pained, and commented, "No preface? That would be like failing to fluff your hair when the door bell rings or not clearing your throat when you've something important to say. Why—"

"Honey, just write your preface so we can have a good home-cooked dinner. Somehow, I've lost my craving for peanut butter sandwiches." (He has always said he could tell how big my inspiration was by the size of the Peter Pan jar I bought.)

And so, dear reader, let this preface be the bridge I've constructed to take you gingerly by the hand from book cover into content. Bits and pieces of my heart and slices of our life, Gene's and mine are revealed within these pages. This is a book of lessons learned, most of them the hard way, as well as dealings we've had with others along life's peopled paths. It is a book of musings (and hopefully, some will be amusing).

It is my earnest prayer that the Spirit of God will move upon your heart as you read these chapters. Now may the love of God the Father, and of the Son, and of the Holy Spirit be with you. And with His kind permission, may the love of Char and Gene Potterbaum flow into your heart alongside His warm and generous and perfect love.

THANKS LORD, I NEEDED THAT!

1

I'd like my opening paragraph to be as thrilling as the opening scenes from *Sound of Music*, but the only thing I have to inspire me is the sound of my dishwasher, and believe me, that's like the sound of music to *my* ears, but doesn't do a thing for paragraph one—or my reader either, for that matter.

And so, as I was burning the most recent wastebasket full of opening paragraphs in the fireplace, I decided that people, being basically romantic the way they are, might enjoy the tender (if somewhat awkward) love letter I wrote to Gene on our twenty-fifth wedding anniversary. He was on a sales trip to Colorado, and this was the only way I could convey my feelings to him. The fact that he had no forwarding address posed a problem, so I put c/o 26643V (that happens to be his license plate number) on the envelope and propped it by his bed pillow, awaiting his return.

To my darling husband—
The children are all bedded down, so things are reasonably quiet here at the Trauma Center at 1440. I'm sitting here in rollers with a button missing from my housecoat and not exactly a semblance of the size eleven bride who met you at the end of that aisle just a short twenty-five years ago today. Well, after last Sunday's anniversary party the kids gave us, are you ready to go for a second twenty-five? (I mean years, dear. Not kids.)

All our lovely silver gifts are shimmering in the hutch. I had a few moments of panic when I realized that I may have to give up paper plates forever—they'd never go with all that elegance staring back at me through the glass doors. When I wrote the thank-you notes, I told the givers (those who I knew would take it right) that I "wanted to thank you for the lovely silver gift. Polishing it might revive a few swear words from the past, but with time I'd forget who sent it to me."

I dread the day when Jamie discovers we got two silver trays exactly alike. I know he will want to use them for cymbals! He has already asked for that beautiful pewter plate to go with his Civil War canteen!

And Gene, the pictures came back already. Do you realize we have *six* children? I didn't realize we were so many until I saw all of us together—for now Don is no longer Don, but Don-and-Barb; and Jan isn't just Jan anymore, but Jan-and-Terry—for "the two of them" are all becoming "one"—and to think that our first grandbaby will be here in May, Lord willing!

Yes, sweetheart, time marches on. To me, you are even more handsome in maturity than you were as a young man, for maturity has settled in and given you a look of wisdom that is foreign to youth because it is only developed through experience. My heart went a bit atwitter as it always does when I see you—or your picture—because we learned the value of keeping romance alive through all those rigorous years. Gene, do you think the kids understand that? Do you think they know that romance is just as important in the "forty-years" as it is in the courting years? May we always be the example they need.

As always, it was a bit hard facing up to the fact that I still have a weight problem. Let's face it, sitting for hours in front of a typewriter gets you mostly skinny fingers and a fat fanny! The era we live in caters so to svelte shapes and looking absolutely emaciated in order to be glamorous, it's hard to think that I'd have been "in" only during the Renaissance, when looking "healthy" was in vogue. And so, my darling, I'll continue working steadfastly on inner beauty by doing all I can with the help of the Holy Spirit to develop a "quiet spirit" and a "grateful heart"; and I will pray that you, my darling husband, will not mind too much if the quiet spirit and grateful heart I develop is imprisoned in a rather "well-padded cell."

How I praise God for the thrill I get when you slip your hand into mine, for the reverence I feel when I look your way, for these twenty-five years and six children He has given us. How comforting it is to know that He holds the future in His hands. We need have no dread of what tomorrow holds, for His thoughts toward us are only for our good, no matter how unexplainable the circumstances might seem to us.

And clearly, there is one fact that must be faced. If the Lord does not come before too long, we will all say goodbye to one another at different times. Life should be a preparation for just this one thing: that we all live one day at a time, realizing our loved ones are only loaned to us for as long as the Master sees fit. Have we prepared our little ones enough? Have we sufficiently stressed the importance of being rooted in the Eternal, so that when frail human relationships break down, or are removed, they will still have a foundation which cannot be moved?

But this one thing I know, that "becoming one" has often been painful—but so worth it. And how balancing "becoming one" is! I remember that you were sometimes too much in a shell as a young man, and I was too noisy and talkative. Now I am more quiet and subdued, and you are never in a shell anymore. There is a manly, godly strength about you that others are noticing. And isn't it exciting to know that as you reflect the glory of God, I am more able to reflect *your* glory? For the Bible says that man is the glory of God and woman is the glory of the man! It is actually possible to "catch" His reflection from you!

And Gene, I know it hasn't always been easy. You married me when I was still a child, emotionally. Thank you for helping me to grow up. Thank you for enduring the growing pains. Thank you for believing the waiting would be worth all the trouble I've caused you. Thank you for being patient with me, like the times I pouted when you took me to the midget races and I showed obvious disappointment because they weren't *really* midgets racing. Thank you, too, for loving me when I made out those checks wrong at the store because I thought "clearing the machine" meant tearing off the tape!

Thank you for buying the second pair of eyeglasses in six weeks because toddler Markie slipped mine into the tea kettle without my knowing it, and I made you instant coffee laced with resin and banana oil. Those glasses looked as if they'd been wadded up in someone's fist! Remember how we laughed? Even when you recalled that it amounted to a fifty-two-dollar cup of coffee, you still laughed. Not many husbands would have!

Please hurry home. We are waiting for you. God bless you, dear husband.

Love, Char

2

It's going on twenty-six years now, and Gene is still waiting patiently for the perfect egg. I've presented him with eggs that have been laced, filigreed, runny, oblong, hard, but never "just right." On "egg mornings" it's like a ritual. He is hanging over my shoulder, breathlessly watching to see what this egg will bring forth. Once I told him to go out and shop around for a perfect chicken. Maybe that would help.

One morning, as we were both peering into the skillet, whispering, "This is it!" the telephone rang. Enter, another harried housewife. Exit, one perfect egg.

I'll call her Evvie, for no other reason than that isn't her real name. I guess you could say she found her way into my life through my first book. It seems her mother-in-law, who lives in another state, read my book and discovered that Evvie and I live in the same neighborhood. She called her daughter-in-law and encouraged her to get in touch with me, so we made arrangements to meet.

Poor Evvie. She'd been a nervous wreck waiting for me to make my appearance at her doorstep. Little did she know that I was struggling with the same basic feeling of panic. Few would ever believe that meeting new faces is difficult for me, but it is. There is often a momentary temptation to give in to the old fear of rejection that used to overwhelm me. But I praise God that the feeling is only momentary, and He quickens to me that I am His, and that He has called me to this ministry.

And so, there must always be an icebreaker. Usually I trip over the front doormat. Sometimes I bend over a playpen and pat their little one, remarking what a handsome boy he is—only to find out his name is Mary Lou.

But this time, I put her at ease by telling her, when she asked me where I'd like to sit, that I really felt more at home closer to her coffee pot. To this she replied flatly, "I don't have one." So we just kind of looked at each other and giggled and I muttered something to the effect that "maybe I should have packed a sack lunch." Which finally put her at ease and we settled for tea, instead.

Evvie soon revealed that her husband had left her just three weeks prior to my visit. As I looked around her tastefully decorated home, so neat and clean, and saw how trim she was, and how pretty, I couldn't help asking myself, "Why?"

We women let ourselves in for this trap so often. We think that being beautiful is all that is required to hold the affections of a man. We think this even more strongly if we don't happen to be endowed with great natural beauty ourselves. My thinking had been so molded by having always felt as a child that if you looked just right, wore the very best clothes, were beautiful and shapely, only then could you be happy. This is no reflection on my parents because I don't think they instilled this into me. It just seems to be something you acquire while you are growing up. I struggled with these feelings of inferiority all my life. (Actually, the only thing I had going for me as a child was my dimples, so I smiled a lot. Praise God, it's become a way of life.)

But I had come to Evvie as a friend. As she talked, my heart began to ache with the age-old ache. Here sat another rejected young wife with no idea of how she had failed to meet her husband's needs. She frankly admitted she couldn't whole-heartedly give any admiration or praise to him because she was quite sure she'd never get any in return. (Oh, such a little seed of love, in the hand outstretched that says, 'I'll give you just one tiny bit of love, but you're going to have to show me that I'll get it back before I give some more!'") And how God's heart is saddened, for He knows He cannot break one of His eternal laws—and His law says that "what you sow, you reap." If you sow a shallow first-let-me-see-what-I-get-in-return love, you are going to reap that same kind of thin love.

Evvie related some deep things, and also some of the more trivial things. Her husband wanted her to wear her hair long and flowing; she hated messing with it and wanted it short for the sake of convenience. He liked his mustache; she despised it. She couldn't see why she should have to mess with long hair if he wasn't willing to shave that monstrosity off his face.

She admitted she nagged quite a bit, specially in the area of his not spending enough time with her and the children, and of working too many hours. She thought he was too strict, that he overdisciplined the kids. He spent his money on things she didn't approve of (although she admitted he was a good provider) and she didn't like his friends. She couldn't figure out why he wasn't handier around the house—like his father.

She complained that any time she made a special effort to get dressed up, he never noticed. I could see that only much prayer and much wisdom could untangle this mess. After she had ventilated for a while and I could get the ''feel'' of the situation, it seemed to be my turn to talk.

I said, ''Evvie, I have a task that will require great love and understanding on your part. First, let me make myself very clear. I know that both of you are equally responsible for these problems. But you see I have a problem, too. Somehow, I must get one of the two of you to be willing to draw a circle around yourself and confess, ''Lord, I cannot change the other person. Give me the willingness and the grace to allow *You* to change *me*. Help me to see where I have been wrong.''

I saw her wince a little, but I continued. ''Evvie, I'm asking you to be that willing one. Oh, there is a price to be paid. You'll hurt terribly on the inside at times. You will be asked by the Lord to do things *His* way, not yours; and you will not be able to give in to the unkind words you feel popping into your mind. And the only way to carry this whole thing off is to establish a richer relationship with Jesus Christ than you have now.''

She looked a bit wide-eyed, but she asked, ''Where do I begin?''

''First you must determine in your heart that you want Christ to be Lord of your life. Then you need to get better acquainted with Him. You can do this by listening to what He has to say in the Bible. Then you need to talk with Him. You'll feel a bit silly at first, trying to carry on a conversation with someone you can't even see—but hang in there. I assure you that He does hear you, and those fumbling words you utter will be as pleasing to Him as baby talk is to a mother. And if you feel a bit silly talking out loud, then just whisper. And don't be afraid to shed some tears if you feel like it. Tears have a great therapeutic, cleansing quality about them. If you are truly sorry about all the wrong things you've done, you'll welcome the tears.''

I stirred my tea. ''The next thing you have to determine is that you are going to accept your husband just the way he is.''

She interrupted with, ''Look, this will never work! We *both* have to change! I don't—''

Having come from a long line of interrupters myself, it wasn't hard for me to do just that. ''No, let me continue. You can hit me later when I've finished my tea.''

I went on, praying inwardly in the Spirit. ''Evvie, I will never forget the time when Gene and I were having one of our 'discussions.' This was a number of years ago, when I seemed to be wallowing around in immature attitudes from my self-righteous pedestal. I really don't remember what I'd been complaining about, but as long as I live I will never forget the hurt look on his face when he said to me, 'Char, why can't you be satisfied with me just the way I am?' And he turned around and went upstairs. If I'd been more sensitive to his needs and less self-centered, that could have been the start of a new relationship for us. But no, I had to go on being 'God's little helper.' ''

It was almost time for our children to come home from school, so I got up to leave, telling Evvie I'd be back in a few days.

So often I have the feeling that I am only repeating myself when I talk with others. But human nature is basically the same and I believe that all our problems are spiritual ones. So, if there is a problem it is because some basic law of God has been disobeyed, and usually disobeyed in ignorance. People today are just not really aware of God's laws, how they work, why they work. The average man on the street could tell you about Noah's ark and

Jonah and the whale but couldn't tell you why his marriage is going flat. It's often simply because he has no understanding of God's principles.

You see, there is no hope for us apart from Jesus Christ. There is no change that is real and lasting apart from Him. But more than just a nodding acquaintance is needed. The Bible tells us that we should love the Lord our God with all our hearts and souls and strength and mind. And Christ is the cornerstone of such a foundation of love—not a vague Christ, but a living, vibrant, miracle-working, prayer-answering Christ. Anything or anyone less will not do.

And out of an established, ongoing love relationship with Christ will flow all the attitudes that are necessary to carry out a loving obedience to His Word.

I had told Evvie that she should accept her husband just the way he was. What Scripture is that based on, you ask? It's based on the Scripture that says we should "do unto others as we would have them do unto us." Now if you will examine your own heart, you will 'fess up to the fact that it is a burning desire of your heart to be accepted for what you are, *just* as you are. There is nothing more unsettling than being in the presence of someone who doesn't like you the way you are. And do you see how this same principle can apply to your children? Every "don't do this, don't do that" says, "I disapprove!" (My poor son, Don, thought for sure his name was "Donnie-don't" until he went to school.)

As a counselor of young women, I sometimes feel as though I'm walking a tightrope. On the one hand, it is necessary to make them see their need for Christ. But on the other hand, it is absolutely necessary to make them see that this is a personal experience, one that cannot be thrust on others with an attitude of "Now that I have this I am undoubtedly better than you; therefore you must have this and become like me!"

Yes, I must present Christ to them, and yet I must protect the husband's freedom to come to this decision in his own time. It must be his own choice, not something he is being coerced into just to get his wife off his back.

Now, see if you can follow: Imagine Christ shining in all His goodness and love. Next, you will picture a young couple. God has

11

just spoken to this young wife's heart and convinced her that she needs to come to Christ, acknowledging Him as her Savior. The light and love of Christ dawn on her and she is basking in His love, eagerly awaiting an opportunity to tell the whole world (specially her husband) about this wonderful experience she has had. (And praise the Lord, that's as it should be! I am always a bit suspicious about anything less than a truly dynamic encounter with Christ.)

But do you see what's happening? She's left the husband out there in the cold! Suddenly, he has lost his wife to someone he can't see who, instead of becoming his friend, has become his rival! The same wife who used to go places with him has turned him into a baby-sitter while she runs off to meetings, to be "blessed." Not wanting to feel guilty about keeping his wife home from something that will make her a better person, he says little or nothing but begins to build up resentments on the inside that show up in the most subtle ways. (Please realize I know this road well, having traveled it before!)

Suddenly, said wife feels that her Christian brothers and sisters are exceedingly interesting because they talk about the things she enjoys the most—spiritual things. She finds a great lack in her own husband and doesn't know what to do about it. A communication gap sets in. What can we do about it? Well, we can set out to deal as gently and tenderly with these erring wives as we know how.

First, we must get them to see their husbands in an entirely new light. We must help them to see that their husbands have been created in the image of God just as they have been, and that these unsaved, disinterested husbands are loved by God in their unlovable state just as God loved these young wives in their most unlovable condition before they came to Christ! How quickly we forget that we were lavished with this unconditional love that says I loved you just as much in your unregenerate state as much as I love you now in your newness of life. Don't we have a tendency to say that surely God loves me more now that I am so much better? And then we have a way of looking down our self-righteous noses and concluding, "God couldn't love him. Why, he smokes. He drinks. He uses bad language. And I don't approve of these things."

And God grieves.

So what is the remedy? The remedy lies in getting them to

13

realize that that husband of theirs has not only a bad side, but a good side as well—just like themselves. The next step is to get them to take the "bad side" of their husband and face it toward Christ's love.

You see, only the love of God can deal properly with our bad side, anyhow! Then, allow your husband's *good* side to face toward *you*. As you line up your love for Christ with a growing reverence for your husband (for this will be the outcome), and as you concentrate on his good points, leaving the bad side for the Lord to handle, you'll stop mentioning his bad points to your friends, and specially to him. The grand result will be that you will begin to point up the good qualities that he has, and you will cause yourself to be grateful to the Lord for giving you such a good husband. You'll actually begin to admire him! He has a great craving for this admiration, but his masculine ego will not allow him to verbalize this need.

Let me share with you what the Amplified Bible has to say about this neglected word "reverence." In Ephesians 5:33 we find the words "let the wife." Notice it doesn't say, 'I will cause the wife." No, God places the responsibility squarely on *our* shoulders by saying, *"Let* the wife *see* that she respects and reverences her husband—*that she notices him, regards him, honors him, prefers him, venerates and esteems him; and that she defers to him, praises him, and loves and admires him exceedingly"* (italics mine).

Now, I suppose it would be more kind of me to stop here, but according to the Amplified, that is only the beginning. In 1 Peter 3:2 we read: ". . . together with your reverence [for your husband. That is, you are to feel for him all that reverence includes]—to respect, defer to, revere him; [revere means] to honor, esteem (appreciate, prize), and [in the human sense] adore him; [and adore means] to admire, praise, be devoted to, *deeply love and enjoy* [*your husband*]" (italics mine).

The Bible says that a man should "love his wife." Evidently God knows that her deepest craving is to be loved. And, as the Bible says that she is to "reverence" her husband, which carries with it all these mystifying undertones of admiration, I guess one could safely conclude that this kind of admiration must be a deep-seated need within the hearts of our males, or God wouldn't have stressed so emphatically that we satisfy that need!

Once my husband made a remark about "women hurting their husbands' pride." Then he added a bit apologetically that maybe that was all right, since pride was something Christians were to root out. But after a moment's reflection he pondered, "But again, I'm not so sure. The pride that has to do with arrogance and haughtiness should be squelched but not the masculine ego. I should have said that when women smash their husbands' masculine ego, the damage is almost irreparable." Now, if God said it in His Word and my husband said it from his heart, who are we to argue?

3

I came across this story one day when I was doing my best to "take pleasure in necessities" such as cleaning out drawers.

It is the graphic story of Gene and me and my precious "unwanted baby." Shocked? You needn't be. Because, like so many other things in my life, this terrible attitude that governed me has turned out for the Lord's glory. The "unwanted baby" loved to hear this story when she was little because she sensed that I was being honest with her, and she knows it has a happy ending.

A tear slipped down my cheek. It ran along the faded blue housecoat and into the greasy dishwater. I leaned heavily against the sink. The tears, coming now in rapid succession, spelled death to the last remaining suds.

Every glance at the greasy abyss caused a fresh wave of nausea to roll over me. I was certain now of what I had tried to ignore for days.

"I'm going to have another baby." I spoke the words slowly, deliberately. I wanted the words to bring back memories of tiny dimpled fists of a helpless little infant nestled in my arms. The words only trailed into thin air, leaving vivid recollections of the discomforts that would be ahead: long periods of morning sickness; the increased irritability that always accompanied my pregnancies; the top-heaviness; the swelling; labor itself. (My first two weighed only ounces under ten pounds.) No, the thought of another pregnancy held no thought of joy for me.

The pans that had been allowed to stand overnight were as weary of the struggle without suds as I was. Changing water meant exertion. I placed the greasy skillets in the oven. They would have to wait for either renewed vigor or a husband's touch. Releasing the culprit water down the drain caused the nausea to be a very real thing. I covered my mouth and dashed to the bathroom. A voice sleepily mumbled from the depths of the pillow he was hugging, "Are you all right?" At that particular moment, I had no intention of being even the least bit civil to him.

"Of *course* I'm not all right!" I snapped. "I'm pregnant!" And with this profound announcement, I leaned against the tub and sobbed convulsively. I suppose I did it for his benefit, that he might somehow be made to feel as miserable as I thought he deserved to feel. He muttered something that was supposed to be soothing, then rearranged himself more comfortably in his pillow. The announcement didn't seem earth-shattering to him.

The commotion had awakened my three-and-a-half-year-old, Larry, and Donnie, my eighteen-month-old baby. Their tummies related a message to them quite different from mine but no less insistent, and they began clamoring for their breakfast. Friend husband asked politely if I could please quiet the din in the kitchen as he intended to sleep another hour or so.

As I made my way back to the kitchen I tried to still my inward rage. I wanted to shout, "Well, *I'd* like to sleep in some Sunday morning, too. I'm the one who is pregnant, remember?" Half-blinded by bitter resentment and a bit weakened by the nausea, I nearly fell over the basket of unironed clothes that had accumulated. My children shrieked with delight and my husband just burrowed deeper into his pillow.

Again, hot tears began coursing their way down my flushed cheeks. Slamming cupboard doors didn't seem to ease my hurt even a little bit, but I was certain it rankled his envied repose, so I went at it with a passion.

The thought of another bout with nausea caused me to quickly change the breakfast menu from greasy bacon and eggs to cold cereal, hot chocolate, and a vitamin pill. Besides, the cereal was crunchy and would keep them busier, longer.

17

I took advantage of the temporary quiet broken only by their munching and an occasional battle cry and went in to the living room to rest.

It didn't make me feel any better. Yesterday's papers were strewn all over. Toys were scattered here and there. Ashtrays were heaped from last night's company, sending forth a most unwholesome odor. The curtains were limp and badly in need of sudsing. The entire house held a hint of decay no matter where I looked. I decided I'd probably feel better in the kitchen. At least the skillets were out of sight.

As I entered the kitchen, the hot chocolate boiled over on the burner I had forgotten to turn off. I did what I could to fan the offensive odor toward Sleeping Beauty, then began to dab aimlessly at the scorch-scented rivulets running down my range.

What I saw from the side window didn't make me feel any better. The neighbor's children, all Sunday shined and crisply starched, were playfully pushing each other toward the car. I couldn't help wishing at least one would tumble into the mud beside the driveway. Nothing could please me more than seeing them late for church at least once.

Their mother had a knack for organization that irritated me. I resented her genuine friendliness. She was never ruffled and always had her children under control. I had even resented the freshly baked cherry pie she brought over the day we moved in. And now, I resented her God.

There had been no religious training in my childhood, but there were memories, when as a teen-ager . . . oh, what was it? What had happened? Something kept me from remembering. I could only be aware of how intensely I disliked loud preachers, hard pews, gospel quartets, or gospel anything.

The months wore on and, as nature would have it, the nausea wore off—only to be replaced by a ravenous appetite. But something remained that frightened me. *I didn't want that baby.* I hadn't felt this way during the other pregnancies. I'd heard about mothers who rejected their children and I was afraid I'd become one. A heavy burden of guilt began to weigh me down.

I tried desperately to analyze my feelings and to gain complete control of my thought life. Materially, I had everything going for me. My husband was adorable and patient, a very good provider. My children were healthy and robust, if a bit unruly. My home was more than adequate. Still, I continued to cry more than I cared to admit.

Valiantly, I tried to lead a normal life. I went to club and continued to dazzle them with my off-color wit and slightly tarnished sparkle. I thought that by making others laugh, I could somehow compensate for the emptiness, the void that needed filling.

The young mother next door was still bothering me. Every time I saw her bustling purposefully about, my own inefficiency loomed before me like an unconquerable foe.

But one day something happened. I don't know how, but it happened. There were no flashes of lightning, no thunderings from heaven, no angelic visions. Only an overwhelming, sudden realization that I didn't need my neighbor's composure as much as *I needed her Christ*. I was sure that He must be the source of her peace. She knew God, and I didn't. This had to be the difference.

And so, right in the middle of my living room I lifted my tear-stained face toward heaven and cried, "I need God!" It was as simple as that! He met me right then and there at my point of need. I embraced Him rapturously as memories began flooding my consciousness once again of the fervent teen-ager who had freely cried as God touched her mightily and placed a call on her life at the "laying on of hands" ceremony after her water baptism.

But that was in the past. Yes, I had "gone my own way." I had steered away from the things of God. But there in my living room I was face to face with the God of the present who could use me *where* I was, who loved me *as* I was. Oh, what peace flooded my tattered soul! With this confrontation came a keen desire to read His love letters to me. The Bible! Where was it? The attic! I'd seen it years ago when I was looking for my wedding dress. Yes, I was sure it was there.

What a sight that must have been for the Lord to behold. Me, the one with a call on my life, the one who had turned my back on Him (supposedly forever), the scoffer, the one who had ridiculed spiritual things—that same person turning the attic upside down in search of a yellowed Gideon Bible that no doubt had been taken by

19

someone from a motel room years ago. (Many thanks, Gideons!)

From that moment, delightful things began happening to me. I fell in love with life again! I nearly hugged the children to death. And needless to say, that baby within me became the object of many heartfelt prayers. The tears continued, but they were cleansing tears of repentance. I couldn't wait to hold her. (Someone said, "Her? What makes you so sure?" I replied, "Because I read in the Bible that He knows what we have need of even before we ask it, and I think our home needs a girl.")

Then one day, when the "fullness of time" had come, they laid a beautiful ten-pound (again!) bit of humanity in my arms, as lovely a rosebud as I had ever seen. I was very tired, but I took *her* little hand in mine and whispered, "Welcome to this world, little Janis Elaine." I hugged her close to me as I fell off to sleep, never realizing that "Janis" meant "Gift of God."

But just as I drifted off to sleep, I murmured, "Thanks, Lord—I needed her."

4

I don't think it is so much a matter of getting out on the wrong side of the bed as much as it is a matter of getting out on the wrong side of an attitude or the wrong side of the alarm clock.

Now, at the risk of your thinking that I'm trying to prove my spirituality, I'd like to say that my day goes more smoothly if I get up while the little hand is still on the right-hand side of the alarm clock, say around five-ish. Before you "oo" and "ah" at my great fortitude, let me just say that I need a two-hour advantage over the rest of the clan to determine whether or not my heart is even beating. Slow metabolism, I think someone called it. It takes me this long to do away with that wooden feeling that makes me walk like a robot. It gives me time to see which is going to start perking first, my blood or the coffee pot.

If I haven't had those two hours to get my thinking clear and my attitudes straight (via some time with the Lord), I'm apt to fall into the trap that awaits every slow-thinking mother as she yawningly approaches various bedrooms mumbling, "What do you want for breakfast?" Simultaneously from three different bedrooms the kids bellow, "French toast!" "Bacon and eggs!" "Coco-wheats!" and you sleepily realize you just blew it. If you give in to any one choice of the three, they will spend the first twenty minutes haranguing you about loving that particular one more than the others.

The next twenty minutes will be spent in bickering about who has to wear the most, the oldest, the grubbiest hand-me-downs.

For instance, the other morning, Mark was sullenly remarking that Jamie didn't have it so bad; at least *his* hand-me-downs came from a *brother*. This was accompanied by a glare at Laurie, his elder next-of-kin. But I made Mark aware of the fact that he really didn't have it so bad either, as all girls were now wearing boys' clothes. This was accompanied by a motherly sigh as I ruefully glanced at my dazzling sixteen-year-old maiden sipping hot chocolate in bib-overalls and denim shirt, with only two pert hair ribbons and a curvaceous figure for a dead giveaway.

Yes, the two-hour head start (I suppose I could be poetic and call it "heart start") has been a great discipline for me. These two hours are also fine for remembering any gym suits that need to be washed or torn pockets that need to be mended. It is also fine for stepping squarely before the mirror and facing the facts of life.

Here is my formula:

First, I wash my face and brush my hair. Then I cautiously open one eye while mustering up the courage to open the other one. When both eyes are as fully wide open as only small, beady, thinly lashed eyes can be, I then brush my hair again. Right, this time. Then, I audibly state that "This is the day that the Lord hath made. I will rejoice, and be glad in it." Then while brushing my teeth, I praise God for all the good things He's given me: my husband, my children, my home, my health, my salvation, my responsibilities.

And then I become very practical. While I'm dressing, I give all of these things back to Him one by one. Internally, I say, "Lord, You've given me all these things but never let me lose sight of the fact that they are really Yours and only loaned to me. Father, I give to You again my rights to my husband. Because he is Yours, and is being guided by You, I will do nothing to interfere with Your plan for his life. I will not try to be his conscience, nor point out his faults. I will do everything I can to make our home a happy place for him. I will not whine and complain because his time is taken up by others or that he often has to be gone many days at a time. I will enjoy him while he is home and accept his being on the road as from Your hand. I thank You, Lord, for his imperfections. You have asked him to give up his dream of having a perfect wife in order to live with me, so I hereby relinquish my dreams of a perfect husband so that I can realistically relate to him. I give up my rights to his time and attention, and if out of Your goodness You give me some of his time, I will accept it from Your hand as a privilege. I promise to refuse all thoughts of self-pity if his business demands rob me of him. In essence, I'm asking You to arrange all the circumstances of this day according to Your lovingkindness. And because I trust Your judgment, I will accept all of the circumstances for this day as coming from You, believing You to be the blessed controller of all things. I promise to accept the circumstances not as I wished they were, or even as they should be, but *as they are*. I will accept my husband the way he is and my children the way they are, praying earnestly that they will do the same for me.

"Father, I confess to You that vain imaginings only rob me of energy and spiritual vitality, so I will continually bring each of my thoughts captive unto the obedience of Christ. I will do all this in Jesus' name and for His sake. Amen."

By that time, my metabolism will have caught up with my spirit and the two will be flowing together. I can then go to the Word, enjoy my time with Him, and have freshly brewed coffee along with my spiritual meat. No oppression dares come near me. And then, at seven, when the droves of little ones (and the larger ones, too) descend on me, I feel certain they will somehow absorb my attitudes by some remarkable spiritual osmosis. The Bible says that "God hath anointed thee with the oil of gladness," and I'm convinced that *the oil only flows down!* I know that my attitudes have become right because of that time spent with Him. As I go about preparing breakfast, I can hug the memory of the "secret place" to me and whisper, "Thanks, Lord—I needed that."

23

5

About a week and a half ago Larry, my eldest son, walked in here and nonchalantly stuck a partially filled can of beer in my refrigerator. It was almost as if I could hear the Lord saying, "Testing—one-two-three—testing." And I got the message.

I went on about my business as though he'd been doing this for years. We were not accustomed to having alcoholic beverages in our refrigerator, but as I didn't see any bolt of lightning from the heavens, I couldn't see that any great damage had been done.

But that was a week and a half ago, and in that time even the finest beer couldn't hold up in anyone's refrigerator against the fumes of a garlicky casserole and a soggy box of turtlefood. Then there was the added fact that several dear Mennonite ladies were about to converge on me (they'd *never* understand the presence of a beer can in the refrigerator) and so I felt the period of testing was over. I began to pour the remaining beer down the sink—only to have the can slip out of my hands and smack-dab into the center of the garbage disposal where not even the slimmest, daintiest fingers could ever reach, grip, clutch, or throttle.

I thought if I was to wet the end of a rubber-tipped dart, just maybe I could ease the disturbing nuisance out of the disposal. So I hunted all over the house for a rubber-tipped dart, but after peeking through every frond of my potted ferns, and after breaking two fingernails from scrunching my hands down between the couch cushions, I finally decided that all darts had been broken or disposed of. The thought persisted, though, that I'd seen one recently.

About this time, the doorbell rang. There stood a lovely young woman. She said almost apologetically, "Oh, I know this is most unusual, but Dr. McGill, your neighbor"—she was pointing across the street and down the block a few houses—"said he knew you'd be more than willing to talk to me, and I'm so desperate. Can you take a few minutes to talk?"

I replied, "Of course I can. Come in. But how did you find me? How did you know where I live?"

She explained, "Well, I want so much to believe that the Holy Spirit led me here, but I think maybe the tennis shoe on your roof had something to do with it. I forgot to ask Dr. McGill which house was yours, but I'd heard him say you had several children, and somehow, this looked—"

"Say no more, and do come in. But tell me, what else did Dr. McGill say?"

"Well, he said you'd be willing to talk—said you'd love it."

I couldn't help giggling. She asked, "What's wrong?"

I said, "Nothing. It's just a standing joke that we have. Dr. McGill and I have never met; yet, from having read one another's books, we feel as though we know each other quite well. You do know that he's also written a book, don't you?"

"Oh, yes! That's why I called him. I thought he'd be just the right one to talk to my husband. But after I'd talked a few moments and told him the problems I was having with my husband, he said, 'No, I have a better idea. You go talk to my neighbor.' You know, I can hardly believe that you live across the street from one another, have both written a book of letters and have shared these books with each other, and yet you've never met!"

We'd moved into the kitchen by now and I was still trying to remove the offensive beer can from the disposal. I was bent over the sink, so I said, "Honey, he has much wealth, prestige, and his mission field is the country club set. Me? I have a gym shoe on my roof, crab grass, and a beer can stuck in my disposal. Our common bond is Christ, and we both feel some day God will set up our first meeting—quite by accident.

By now she was intently engaged in watching me try to remove the beer can. Finally, in a burst of absolute genius I exclaimed,

"Scotch tape! A big fat ball of sticky tape! That should do it."

With that, I reached into a drawer, made a thick wad of Scotch tape, and very carefully lifted the can out, pitching it into the trash. We still had some time left before the Mennonite ladies were to arrive, so we went on with our somewhat disjointed conversation.

It wasn't long until I discovered why God had moved Dr. McGill to send her to me. As is so often the case, her problem was not with her husband. Her problem was her own wrong attitude toward her husband, her inability to see him in proper perspective. And also, she'd fallen into the trap of "the Bible was written to Christians, so none of these things apply to my unsaved husband. Therefore I don't have to submit to him."

I think it took a good half hour of searching the Word together, combined with a patient showing forth of His love through her outbursts of "But you don't understand. I can't submit—he doesn't even know the Lord."

Suddenly, I saw at exactly what moment the Holy Spirit spoke the Word to her heart. It was as though a million-watt bulb had lit up within her! She fell back against the chair, murmuring, "Oh, no! Now I see! I've been doing it completely wrong all this time! You mean I'm to see him as the one through whom Christ will speak to me, even though he is unsaved? That I can still trust God to give me direction through him, even if he doesn't know the Word? That being good and kind to my husband is the same as being good and kind to Christ? Oh, I've never treated him like a king. Dear God, will he forgive me? Oh, I have to go; I've got to get home and fix dinner— for the *king*. I'll call you tomorrow!"

And out the door she went, rejoicing. Well, she just had to come back the next day for coffee, she had so much to share with me. She was almost chortling as she burst into the house. "You'll never believe it. God gave me just the right words. I asked his forgiveness for never having treated him like a king. God filled that room and things are so much better." And on and on she went.

At one point she said, "Char, why does God trust us women with this tremendous responsibility of winning our husbands to Himself when He knows very well that most of us start out on the wrong foot by preaching, pushing, and playing God?"

I thought a moment. It was a question I'd often asked myself. "I think it's because His strength is made perfect in weakness. When once we, the weaker sex, learn the difficult lessons involved in such a responsible position, we amply show forth His glory, having learned it the hard way. In no way could we turn to our sisters who are in the midst of the same trials we've come through and tell them that they could do it without the power of God. We know from 'whence cometh our strength.' ''

I was making a casserole at the time. I don't think anyone realizes how difficult this is for me—trying to work and talk at the same time. I'd determined that after I'd added the dry mustard I would stop working and finish the casserole later. I dipped the measuring spoon into the small tin of dry mustard and felt something go "clunk." There before our eyes was a yellow-dusted, long-lost *puzzle piece* sitting in the measuring spoon as though it felt it belonged there.

We burst out laughing. I gave it all up as a bad try, and poured us some coffee. As she was leaving, she pointed toward the ceiling and advised me, all the while trying to keep a straight face, "In case you ever get a beer can stuck in your disposal again, there is the rubber-tipped dart you need!"

I looked upward, and sure enough, big as life, there was the end of a dart sticking out of the overhead hall light fixture. I giggled, "I knew I'd filed it away somewhere—just couldn't remember!"

6

The beer can in my disposal . . . are you still wondering? Well, let me tell you about it. Just a few days after the "beer can" incident, our son, Larry, and his dad had a "confrontation." You see, Larry had moved home a month or so after my first book came out. (Perhaps you are thinking that there is little connection. I'm thinking there is a lot of connection because I'd asked all my readers to pray for Larry—and how I thank you for those prayers! His moving back home was the first link in the chain of events.)

Shortly after his return home, Gene asked me, "Do you notice a difference in Larry? He seems so much more willing to help—more loving, somehow."

I said, "Yes, I've noticed. Sometimes I'm almost afraid to speak above a whisper because I think the Spirit of God is up to something, and I don't want to upset the applecart in my own inimitable fashion."

Yes, Larry moved back home. He seemed to be entering in more as a part of the family. One day, as I was fixing breakfast for him he slipped into the chair where I'd been. It so happened that my Bible was open and propped up on some other books. As I prepared breakfast, from the corner of my eye I could see him reading from Corinthians. I continued with breakfast and said nothing, hummed a bit aimlessly, as I recall. But like Mary of old, I was pondering all this in my heart.

As I was busily turning the bacon, I heard him quietly turning a page. I ventured, "Lord, could it be? A smoking flax, Lord?

Perhaps a bruised reed?'' And then I served breakfast, but nothing was said between us.

That night, after we'd come in from visiting some friends, my youngest son, Jamie, ran up to me, tugged on the sleeve of my coat and with great eagerness pulled me down so he could whisper into my ear. "Mom. I've got a secret! I saw Larry in the family room reading that black Bible of Dad's."

I hung my coat up. "Oh? Isn't that great, Jamie! Do you think God is about to do something for Larry?" He didn't answer as he was already headed back to his car track.

But we noticed that Larry was asking things like, "Are you going anywhere tonight?"

And we'd say, "No, why do you ask? Did you want to have someone over? You can, you know."

And he'd say, "No, it's just kind of nice to have the house all to myself."

But the times when he did have tne house to himself, I'd find a Bible lying open on a footstool or chair. I think it was his way of saying, "Mom, dad, let me do it my own way, in my own timing."

It wasn't too many days afterward that he was reading his Bible openly before us. We acted as though this had been his practice at all times. We never mentioned it, never made suggestions. And we never invited him to go to meetings with us.

Perhaps you are thinking that instant perfection was draped around him. No, quite to the contrary. There were some things that God wanted to surface within all of us before this thing could reach a climax.

The "testing" of the beer cans in the refrigerator—that was important. And then, the need to feel independent of us, and also the blowup about his job (he was working for Gene at the time).

Later, after the blowup and the deep sorrow for having resisted Gene's authority, Larry got drunk. It was his last defiant way of saying, "God? Isn't there some other way? Can't I find it in drink? Must it be in surrender to You?" And God answered, "Try it and see."

The blowup had happened in the morning. Gene's parting words to Larry were, "Son, you will never be happy until you come to grips with God." And with that Larry stalked out.

About supper tme, I heard a stumbling sound outside the back door. It was Larry. I went to the door. Quietly, he admitted, "Mom, I'm drunk."

And I said words that were accompanied by "agape" love. I could feel it. Words that said, "I love you because you're you." It didn't matter to me whether or not he was drunk. What mattered to me was my son, not what he'd done or what he'd been drinking. And I added, "Yes, I know." I put my arms around him and helped him into his bedroom, pulled the shades, kissed him, and tucked him in, much like I used to do when he was little. And somehow he seemed little to me, though he is six-foot-four, because I looked at him through a mother's eyes, I suppose.

My last words just before I closed the door were, "I'll have a pot of coffee ready for you when you get up."

"Thanks, mom. Just a couple hours here, and I'll be okay."

But as it turned out, he slept all night. No one said anything to him about the wrongness or rightness of his actions. Life went on as before, but something was different. He was restless, questioning within, yet unable to seek answers from us.

Oh, people, when will we learn that it is easier to take advice, suggestions, exhortations, from those who are not so emotionally tied to us than it is from those closest to us?

And so, a few mornings later, Larry asked, "Mom, do you know where Mike lives?" (He and Mike had roomed together at one time. Mike had come to Christ a year or so prior to this time.)

Go see his sister, Bobbie; she'll know. You know where she lives."

No more, no less.

I got up at five the next morning. Larry was gone, but he'd left a note. "Mom, I took a few groceries. There is some money for them. Don't worry about me. I'll call in a few days and let you know where I am. I promise to brush my teeth and check the oil" (a standing joke between us from "day one," due to natural parental prodding plus the fact that a couple of engines had blown because he forgot to check the oil).

His note may not seem astounding to you, but to me it said much more than just these few words. To me, it said, "Mom, I'm going to Mike for my answers because he was my best friend." It said,

"This money is my way of saying thanks." It said, "Mom, I'm getting confidence again" because the writing didn't look as insecure as it used to—it looked strong and bold. It said, "Mom, everything is going to be all right." And it said, "Mom, it's time to rejoice." And I did.

During that weekend, Larry gave his heart and his life back to Christ. He also received the baptism in the Holy Spirit. Couldn't you hear them announcing it? The angels, I mean. I did. I heard them in my heart. Oh, I'm not going to tell you that I am so spiritual that I knew exactly at what point and where he did all this. No, I didn't know for sure until he told me. But let's put it this way—I heard them practicing, for their anthems were singing in my heart for what was going to be! And now Larry has truly come home! For as Augustine said, "The home of the soul is in God."

Yes, Larry has *come home*!

7

As my niece, Sue, was tucking her little Jimmy in for the night while they were visiting from out of town, he said, "Mummy, leave the light on, will you?"

Sue said, "Now, Jimmy, that isn't necessary."

"Please, mummy," came the little uncertain cry from beneath the blankets.

"Jimmy, tell you what. We'll turn the light out and play like it is on. Okay?"

A fluffing of blankets and arranging of pillows and the good-night kiss. Just as Sue was gently closing the door, a little voice came from under the mound of blankets. "Hey, mummy, I got a better idea. Why don't we turn the light *on* and play like it is *off!*"

Well, the impact of his reasoning was so great, and so hilarious, I never did hear who played what, and which end of the light won out. But the whole incident reminds me of Pete and Rosie who, when they were married, played like they weren't, and when they weren't, played like they were.

I met Rosie through the first book I wrote. Somehow, my first recollections have to do with hearing her say, "I feel like I know you so well." I didn't know at the time that God was going to use Gene and me to put her feet back on a "right path"; but one day, when I found her mother in my living room in tears, suddenly I knew this was more than a social call, and certainly more than a coincidence.

Her mother needed most of all to talk. She started by asking, "Have you heard? Are you aware that Rosie is considering remarrying Pete? I can't bear it. This religion she has gotten herself into—I don't understand it! What was wrong in simply being a good, believing Catholic? Why does she have to go chasing off to some mysterious meeting? It's just another one of her kicks. I know it is! She has so many things going for her; she could have the pick of the crop! She has talent, a good figure, brains. Why does she want to throw away her life, when he treated her so terribly the first time around?"

A pause for tears, and then more tears. After gaining a bit of composure, she continued. "After all I've done for her. I've helped her meet her bills in these two years they've been divorced. Doesn't she remember that he actually *struck* her?"

In fairness, I quickly got in a "only when he'd been drinking, I understand." But it went unheeded.

"He was absolutely infantile! He only wanted to go out with the boys. He left her night after night. He never could settle down. What makes her think he's going to be any different now?"

"His newfound love for Je—" But I was interrupted.

"He's putting up a front! He's still the same, I know he is! Please, use your influence and tell them not to do this foolish thing! I beg of you, ask them to hold off. Do you realize they are wanting to marry again, immediately?"

By now she had talked sufficiently to have gotten rid of some of her anger and frustration. I took a deep breath and inwardly said, "Lord, here we go!" Outwardly, I spoke firmly but with love. "Elaine, I must tell you my position in this matter. According to the Word of God, I have been commissioned to 'teach the younger women to love their husbands.' Now, if Rosie had come into my life before their divorce, it would have been my responsibility to encourage her to stay with him, inspite of so-called mistreatment and immaturity, in spite of her own lack of understanding of what *her* reactions were doing to *him*. But since they are already divorced, I feel a keen responsibility to move heaven and earth—specially heaven—through prayer, to see them remarried!"

I'm not even really sure she heard me. She just continued on in a

kind of soggy monotone that it would be the end of the world for
Rosie and her little granddaughter, Anne, the end of every chance
of happiness for them both. I could see there was no way of making
her understand that God could change and transform people, could
make them new and vital and tender and loving, that through the
Holy Spirit, Pete could come to truly cherish Rosie and make home
a heavenly place of protection for Rosie and Anne.

I tired to tell her that Pete had accepted Christ because he had
seen such a change in Rosie. Rosie had told me herself that since
she had come to Christ, she had begun to understand why their
marriage had failed; their basic self-centeredness was the problem,
plus wrong attitudes and immature responses. I could see that my
words were falling on deaf ears, so I suggested that we pray.

Rosie's mother said, ''All right. Yes, maybe we should. But
how do we pray? I'm a Catholic and you are—what do they call it?
Well, anyhow, you're not a Catholic. Do we kneel?'' as she stood
up.

''No, that won't be necessary, and my not being Catholic won't
make a bit of difference. Here, just let me take your hand. 'Father,
we come to You right now, and I ask you to speak peace to this
mother's heart.' '' With this, she fell into my arms and began to sob.
I continued, ''Lord, help her to see that You have a plan for Rosie's
life—and for Pete's—and that You desire to bless them in that
plan. May this whole tangled, knotted problem bring honor and
glory to Your name as You unravel these circumstances. Thank
You, Father.''

With this, she straightened up, glanced in the mirror, patted her
hair, said some ''thank yous,'' and drove out of my life, for I have
not seen her since.

But for many reasons I felt a need to keep in touch with Rosie. I
loved her and knew that she needed fellowship. God often speaks
of the ''local church,'' and I think He is pleased when we keep in
touch with those in our own area who love Him. It has something to
do with ''better is a neighbour that is near than a brother far off''
(Prov. 27:10 KJV).

And somehow her mother's plea put me squarely in the middle
of the whole episode. I found out from Rosie that she and Pete had
been married for three years but had been divorced for two. For

most of those two years of separation she had carried around an unforgiving and rebellious attitude toward her former husband. But after she'd been saved and filled with the Spirit, she began to see things through God's eyes. Suddenly she knew that she must forgive Pete for all the misunderstanding, the hurts, and the problems that had passed between them. She really wasn't even thinking in terms of remarriage at first, only forgiveness. But when Pete would come to see their daughter, he noticed a new and different Rosie. He saw her softened, beaming, radiant, and tender. No bitterness anymore, no defiance, no arguing over the least little thing. When he would come to pick little Anne up, at times he found himself not wanting to leave. There was something about Rosie that made him want to stay. Finally he said, "Rosie, what's with you? There is something different about you, and I want to know what it is. I've been asking all around if you've fallen for some guy or something. No one seems to know much about it—except that you sure are different."

Rosie scooped little Anne up into her arms, kissed her, and said, "Honey, go play. Mommy wants to talk to daddy. You can go with daddy in a few minutes. Okay?"

And after little Anne had dashed off to play with her friends, Rosie proceeded to tell him. "Pete, yes, I have fallen in love, head over heels in love with my Creator."

It was almost too overwhelming for Pete. "Rosie! Come off it! You? The life of the party? On some religious trip? You're off your rocker!"

But he kept eyeing her. Somehow, he wanted to believe that what she was saying was true. He wanted so much to believe that these things really happened, that you could find rest, repose, and tranquility in this day and age, in God and one could truly say, "In God we trust." Oh, how he wanted it to be so. But he couldn't trust his own emotions, and he couldn't trust Rosie. She'd told half-truths before, trying to get something for herself. She'd been known to exaggerate and had always been a bit dreamy and unrealistic. No, this was some kick she was on, no doubt.

But as days passed and melted into weeks, Pete sensed that this high was for real. One day he casually mentioned, "Could I go to these 'meetings' you are always talking about? Not that I'm interested, but I think I ought to know what kind of propaganda you're teaching Anne.''

When Pete attended, he could hardly believe what he saw. He saw people worshiping "with their whole heart", he saw people unashamedly raising their arms to heaven. He saw a radiance on faces that he could hardly believe. He sensed the presence of God. He knew this was for reàl, and his heart became hungry for what they had.

But he had built such enormous barriers. He'd dabbled in the occult and needed to be freed from these bonds. He'd been on drugs. He'd done other things that cried out for cleansing. But this Jesus, this precious Jesus, kept wooing him, speaking to him in his innermost being until finally within his heart, he yielded to this gentle Savior and accepted Him—but not without a struggle.

With their new found love for Christ in full bloom, they found a new, unselfish love growing within their hearts for one another. Finally Pete told Rosie that even though he had dated a few girls since their divorce, he'd never been happy, had never been able to feel as though there was anyone else for him. Rosie admitted that she felt the same. And then they knew—knew that beyond a shadow of a doubt they were to spend the rest of their lives together. As they started talking about marriage plans, stars were shining from Rosie's eyes and the glory of the Lord could be seen resting on both of them.

Then came this upsetting reaction of her mother, whom Rosie loved so much. They finally decided that perhaps they shouldn't get married right away; but since they were 'already married in the sight of God,' maybe it would be all right for Pete just to move in with Rosie.

About here, I turned chicken. I found out they were taking marital liberties. They hadn't asked for my advice and they weren't part of our fellowship. So I just threw up my hands and said, "Lord, love 'em—and You deal with 'em." (I trust the Lord has forgiven me for my faintheartedness. Today, thanks to His grace, I would be more forthright.)

I still kept in touch. I felt a bit uneasy about the whole situation and rather upset with my own lack of words to clarify my feelings. Their position was that "we are married in God's sight, and we will be legally married real soon."

And so, a number of weeks went by. One Saturday night, we were in our kitchen enjoying a time of fellowship with Kevin and Cordie, two kids from our church. I heard a commotion at the door and when I got there, Rosie and Anne were just coming in amidst some happy "hellos" to my children.

Rosie pulled up a chair and I poured some coffee for her. She seemed unusually quiet. After a few moments she began to unburden her heart, and being like most women, she did it a bit tearfully. "I shouldn't be bothering you with all this, but I just must talk to someone. Things aren't going so well. Pete hasn't made any mention of blood tests or wedding dates, and it seems like we are fighting a lot. But we both really love the Lord, and seem to be so happy at times. I can't figure out what is wrong. I had so hoped—I wanted so much for us to be a testimony to others. What's wrong?"

Gene waited for her to get it all out of her system, and then he started speaking so gently, oh, so gently, to her. "Rosie, honey, your problem is that you *do* have a testimony, but it is a *tarnished* testimony. The Bible asks us to avoid all appearance of evil, it tells us that we should obey even the civil laws. Yet, you have tarnished your testimony in the sight of your neighbors by living together. You may believe yourselves to be married in the sight of God, but in the sight of your unsaved neighbors, you *aren't* married. Do you see what I'm saying?"

He waited a moment, then went on. "By giving Pete all the rights and joys of marriage, you have lost your bargaining point. You mentioned that he seems to have an unforgiving attitude toward you because of the divorce and misunderstandings that have cropped up during the separation. Has God ever laid it on your heart to ask his forgiveness? Are you willing to have God's will in your life, regardless of what it may cost you?"

With great heartbreak, she sobbed, "Yes, above all else."

Gene queried, "Even if it means giving up Pete forever?"

There was a pause—a pause filled with emotion and great stress. Then she replied, "Yes, even that, but I had so hoped. . . ." Her voice trailed off.

Gene went on to say, "Then this is what you must do. We are

going to pray together and ask God to give Pete a forgiving spirit. Then I suggest that you go to him, ask him forgiveness, and share with him that God has shown you that your testimony has been tarnished by your living together. Tell him that you feel your relationship should be broken off for the time being. Ask his forgiveness for having pushed him in the area of his spiritual life. Tell him that you realize now that you should have been willing for him to grow at *God's* pace, not yours. Share with him that God has a way of wanting things done decently and in order, and you feel a need to cooperate with Him. We'll be praying that all this will be done with a penitent spirit, so Pete will realize the authenticity of what you are saying. Are you ready to do this, Rosie?''

And with this, we all prayed for her. We sang for a while and watched as the beautiful ''songs of Zion'' spoke peace to her shredded soul.

The next day was Sunday. Rosie called and announced, ''Well, I did it! It was one of the hardest things I've ever done in my life, but I feel the peace of God within, and I know what I've done is right. When I left your house, I was going through quite a struggle. I wasn't sure that Gene's advice had been from the Lord. I thought it was just ''flesh and blood'' speaking. But when I began to toss and turn on the bed, I knew I was struggling with the Holy Spirit, that the things Gene had spoken to me were really from the Lord, and God was now wanting obedience from me.

''When Pete came in late from work that night, I told him my whole heart, how I needed to know that he'd forgiven me for the divorce, and that in order for God's blessing to be on us as a family, he'd have to move out until we were married—if he cared to go on with our marriage. I asked his forgiveness for pushiness in the area of spiritual things and told him I was wrong about not seeing the Christ in him, only the Adam. And then it was done. He left without a word. I guess this was a good sign, as any other time he'd have left in a fury of bad words and all that goes with bad tempers. But he just left, quietly. I was heartbroken, but even more so when I saw that he'd left his Bible on the coffee table. I felt as though he'd not only walked out of my life, but out of God's life, too. But about an hour later he came back, looking a bit crestfallen. He just said, 'Forgot my Bible. I'll be here for supper tomorrow night, if

38

that's all right with you.' "

Oh, was it all right! They started "courting" and within two and a half weeks, they were married. The last chat I had with them, they were well into a happy marriage with the blessing of God surrounding them. Pete received the baptism in the Holy Spirit just before they were married and is growing spiritually by leaps and bounds fulfilling his role as spiritual head of his household—which is the way it should be!

All is not peaceful yet with Rosie's mother, but I feel certain that with time she will see that this is a good thing—bring honor and glory to the name of Christ. And someday, she too will rejoice that God has brought them back together.

8

I was standing in the kitchen making out a list of things for my daughter, Laurie, to pick up at the store. I heard Gene coming down the stairs with his suitcase, and knew that he'd soon be leaving town. He dashed into the kitchen, gave me a warm hug, a loving kiss, and he was off. I finished giving Laurie some instructions, then turned quickly away. She asked, "What's wrong, mom?"

"It's nothing, honey. It just makes me sad when dad goes, but I know it's a necessary part of his work." How can you explain to a young girl of sixteen the emotional turbulence that you, a mature woman of forty, feel? How can you explain the wrenching that goes on inside? That as her daddy shifts his gears and pulls out of sight, you, by some power stronger than yourself, must shift dependency from your earthly husband to your heavenly Bridegroom? That all the hurting on the inside must be lifted to Him as a sacrifice of praise? That it takes a few moments to give up your rights to companionship, to human desires?

Perhaps I'm not being fair with her. She may be able to understand much better than I realize. She is almost a woman herself. But then she goes off to do my errands, and the house is very quiet—so peacefully and necessarily quiet. For the Lord of my life knows that I need just a few moments—a few tender moments—while the tears help to cleanse me and assure me of His love and presence. Because, you see, there is always that possibility of "not knowing what a day may bring forth." But I lift my heart to Him, thanking Him and praising Him for whatever the future may hold. I know that my times are in His hands. My loved ones are in His care and keeping; and if He should grant that my husband returns to me, what a privilege that will be. The longing and the emotional upheaval that I experience at these times help me to understand the suffering of those dear women who have been deserted and forsaken by their husbands. It helps me to be tender when I share the grief of a widow, having experienced, even on a small scale, this searing hurt of loneliness.

Sometimes I glance down at my left side, thinking to find "tear on perforated line" written there, because each parting has its particular shock. But after I've recovered from the first wave, I can fall safely into whatever plan God has for me at that time, feeling rather secure and warm all the while, because I know that He has arranged my life in this manner so I could have special times with Him. And I can honestly say, "Thanks, Lord—I needed that."

9

Have you ever had the fear that if you prayed for someone you love to come to Christ, God would have to move in some drastic way to get their attention? The very fact that it is a "fear" should tell us the source from which it comes. We need to constantly remind ourselves that God always moves in love and for His glory. Oh, I'll admit that sometimes it looks as though adversity was the very thing that caused some to come to the Lord. I've heard people say, "I came to Him when I was at rock bottom" or "God really had to put the pressure on to make me see the light." Personally, I think it only *appears* this way. The Bible says, "Despisest thou the riches of his goodness and forbearance and longsuffering; not knowing that *the goodness of God leadeth thee to repentance?*" (Rom. 2:4 italics mine).

But isn't it exciting? To think that His goodness is what moves others, I mean. They don't *have* to wait until tragedy strikes, nor do we have to "fear" that our praying will bring it upon them!

And as living proof, I want to share this incident about Gayle and Laura, for they came to Christ right out of worldly contentment and prosperity. After we'd been introduced, I asked, "Gayle, you said you didn't have any needs, any problems. Why then did you come to Christ?"

And he said a precious thing that spoke excitement and encouragement to my heart. "We came to Christ because He is calling out His people to Himself. It's as simple as that." And I couldn't help blushing a bit, as I had made it sound as though a person couldn't come to Christ without some traumatic experience.

He went on thoughtfully. "Well, it happened like this. A few weeks ago, a tiny woman named Sherri stepped up to me and said, 'May I pray for you?' I tell you, I was absolutely indignant! Why should *she* pray for *me*? I had no problems! We had a good marriage, at least it had been a good marriage until this woman—"

At this point, his wife, Laura, broke in. "Gayle! You make it sound downright criminal!"

He laughed, and said, "Laura, it's the truth! Everything was fine until she took you to that charismatic luncheon."

Laura giggled. "Gayle's right. We've always had a good marriage, but I was so changed after attending that luncheon. I suppose he had every reason to be indignant with her. Really, I'd only gone to the luncheon because it sounded like something different, a little out of the ordinary. It was a great meal, and the speaker was dynamic—I'd never heard anything so powerful in all my life. And after he'd finished speaking, he said, 'Would any of you like prayer?' Well, his message made me think it would be a good idea to have some assurance of my salvation as we'd certainly not been living for the Lord, so I walked up to the front. The speaker didn't ask me anything; he just reached out his hand and said, 'Lord, bless her; and I floated backward. Someone caught me and eased me to the floor, and that was the beginning of a love relationship with the Lord."

"Yeah, a love relationship that scared the living daylights out of me," remarked Gayle. "I mean, here I'd been calling on out-of-town customers all week, looking forward to coming home, when I'm met at the door by this dazzling creature who is all lit up like a light bulb! I knew it was Laura, and yet it wasn't the same Laura I'd left the week before. To tell you the truth, I was shook!"

Laura went on where Gayle left off. "I'm sure he thought I'd become a gibbering idiot. I just couldn't contain everything that had happened to me, and I started spilling it all over the place instead of waiting for God's proper timing. And because I didn't wait, what I had to say was coming on him like a heavy thud. He really started getting angry with God for what had happened to me."

"That's right," added Gayle. "And I was still angry, not only at God but with Sherri, that tiny wisp of a woman who wanted to pray for me. But she was so gentle, so gracious. I can't explain it, but something inside of me just kind of broke, and I said yes. She placed her hands on me, and God met me right there in power and blessing! From then on, I was His.''

We couldn't help laughing at the sight that must have been, for Gayle is a huge, strapping man, and I understand that Sherri stood only about five feet tall.

A week or so later, we were visiting at Gayle's home. While there, a man and his wife came in. Gayle introduced them. ''This is Nate; he's my nephew, but he's more like my brother—he's also my business partner. And this is his wife, Jan.''

Nate said, ''Oh, yes, nice to meet you. Are you in this charismatic—uh, what do you call it—uh, movement? That's it.'' (Putting it that way almost made it sound like a disease!)

I smiled and said, ''It was the halo, wasn't it? Gives me away every time'' Gene just turned his head and groaned. (I was certain to be in for a lecture on the way home!)

Well, I'm happy to tell you that Nate and Jan came to Christ that night also. As they sat around and heard us chattering about all the good things God had done for us, and about His guidance, the Spirit of God seemed to speak to their hearts, telling them that what we were saying was true and that it was theirs for the asking.

Gayle said later, after we'd prayed with them, ''The wonder of it all is that they weren't even seeking, and they always seemed to be happy. But a sparkling Jan contradicted him. ''No, not really,'' she confided. In that quiet utterance, she had spoken a multitude of words. She was quietly attesting to the fact that apart from Christ there can be no real happiness, even if the surface looks smooth. For the human heart hungers for God and longs to make its peace with God, even though the intellect may not be able to put the desire into words. There is that continual gnawing within, that something, that crying out for someone who will understand and will fulfill our deepest longings.

Well, it was a truly rewarding experience. As Gene and I were dropping off to sleep that night, he reminded me of something Charles Simpson said: ''If you get there the same time the Holy Spirit does, He'll make you look real good.''

I grinned contentedly and said, ''Thanks, Lord—I needed that!''

' . . . *that tiny wisp of a woman who wanted to pray for me.*''

10

Whenever I jump out of bed in the middle of the night, Gene just lifts his groggy head from the pillow, smiles sleepily, and mumbles, "Lord bless you, Sweetheart." It always makes me feel like such a heel as I know he thinks some great inspirational thought has gripped me, when it's really only a bout with heartburn.

So last night, while I was drowsily munching on a Rolaid, my mind was busily digesting some thoughts that had come to me about this business of raising adolescents. It runs in my mind that I jotted them down somewhere, but I was so sleepy they probably got filed under "ho-hum" or "z-z-zzzz."

If anyone was to ask me what "adolescent" meant, I think I would respond by saying "a-dull-ascent" while gripping the hand of your little ones as you made your way with them through the murky paths of dimply babyhood into the unstable ways of pimply adolescence, until on yonder brow (your wrinkled one, of course) you could see reflected the faint glimmer of maturity. Yet, that doesn't describe it well either, as it is anything but dull. Numbing, perhaps—but not dull.

About the time I'm convinced that raising boys is more difficult than raising girls, one of my daughters has the audacity to make her way into adolescence and change my mind completely. It seems as though some durable, never-to-be-erased tape is inserted into each child at about age eleven that goes for years and years repeating, "You're yelling at me! *Why* are you always yelling at me!'' The tape can be triggered by tender requests such as, ''Dear, will you set the table, please?'' or you may get an instant replay by merely asking, ''Have you finished cleaning up your room?''

We were all in the car, coming home from church the other day. I quietly announced, ''I forgot to mention that I'm having that mole removed from my upper lip, so I won't be taking any speaking engagements this month.''

Laurie asked, ''How come?''

I said, ''Because I think it would be most distracting to watch a lady speaker wearing a bobbing Band-Aid for a mustache.''

She countered, ''That's not what I mean. How come you are getting the mole removed?'' She said it defensively, as though it might be in the same category as using heroin.

I put my finger on the mole and screwed up my mouth all funny. ''Because sometimes it feels like it's pulling, or could be growing or puckering, or something.''

''Hunh,'' she snorted. ''Fine thing. How would you like to be *me*, and have these ugly old pimples pulling all over your face! You won't take *me* to the doctor!''

I looked at her beautiful, flawless face and decided that either I needed to get my bifocals checked or she needed to wash her bathroom mirror.

Meanwhile, two more adolescents bearing our name stopped their arguing from the back seat as to who was mom's favorite, which one always had to do the most work, and who always got his own way the most just long enough to chime in with ''Yeah, mom. How would you like to have an ugly old face like hers?''

Gene, always the model of placidity, took my hand and assured me that someday they would grow up and then we'd all be friends again, and wouldn't that be nice?

Of course there is always the proverbial question of the ''birds and the bees'' bit: how much to share, how much to tell, what can they handle, and so on. The Lord, knowing our slowness in this area, always seems to arrange circumstances to bring to our attention that there are some things they need to know.

For instance, on a rainy Saturday morning, the boys came to me and said, ''Mick just called and wanted to know if we could show some movies in our basement. He said he'd bring his projector.

Could you run us down to the library to get some films?''

Shrewdly, I bargained with them. ''Tell you what. Yes, I'll take you to the library, and yes, you can show films down there if you will clean up your side of the basement. And just to show you that I'm all heart, I'll clean up my side, too. Deal?''

Deal.

And not being overmeticulous, they finished their side of the basement before I did. As I swooshed fuzz-balls from one side of the basement to the other, and was generally stirring up a lot of silt, I glanced over to their side of the basement and saw that they were being enraptured by statistics about the *Titanic* and I couldn't help feeling all warm and motherly to think that they were being so resourceful by finding such a constructive way to spend their rainy Saturday.

I went upstairs to bake some cookies. A bit later, just after Micky had hurried out of the house, Mark came into the kitchen with a rather troubled look on his face. Jamie came in quietly behind him.

Mark spoke first. ''Mom, what's a stag movie?''

''Why do you ask, dear?'' I managed to squeeze the words from tightly drawn lips as I poured half a bottle of vanilla into the cookie dough.

''Micky started to show one. At least he said that's what it was called. But as soon as I saw what it was going to be, I jumped in front of the projector and flung my arms all around—like this.'' He leaped spread-eagled into the air.

Jamie looked thoughtful. ''Yeah. I probably would have watched it if he hadn't. Thanks, Mark.''

Weakly, I parroted, ''Yeah, thanks, Mark'' as my knuckles turned white from clutching the countertop.

Another nudge from the Lord came just a few days later when my next door neighbor, Toni Decker, came over laden down with one twin under each arm (we call them the Double Deckers) and a large children's book that she casually placed on my counter top. She borrowed some sugar, tossed her head toward the book, and said, ''Say, Char, I'm leaving this book here for you to look over. Your kids have taken a peek or two at it while at my house, and I didn't want the word to get back to you that I was showing them pornographic literature. The book was given to me by my

"Mom, what's a stag movie?"

pediatrician, as my kids have been asking so many questions that I couldn't answer. He said they should read this. Let me know what you think of it, and then do what you want about your kids reading it. Bye now!'' Out she sailed amidst a trail of dogs, babies, and sugar.

Well, it was a book of cartoon sketches with heavy undertones about the birds and the bees, and hilariously well done, I must say, although a bit too graphic to my tastes as the sketches all looked as though I might have posed for them. I know they were just being facetious, but why did they have to strike so close to home?

I read the book, gulping considerably on my way through it. I ignored Gene's remark, ''That's the dirtiest book I ever saw,'' and wondered why we get so squeamish about the facts of life. We know that ''all things work together for good'' and that, after all, God originated this whole business, anyhow. And so after much crimson hysteria we decided that if they had already ''peeked'' at the book, perhaps they should read the whole thing and at least have a foundation as to the facts.

We explained to them that yes, God was the one who thought of this plan, and that really, it was a very good plan, only Satan had managed to wrench it out of its proper place and put it into the hearts of men as something dirty or evil. We did all we could to put it into right perspective, mentioning that although God instigated sex, you still didn't go around talking about it with your playmates. (I could see them making a mental note: ''Unless they've read the book, of course.'')

Something similar happened with Laurie. It was her sixteenth birthday, and due to the excitement and flurry of presents and attention, plus the added thrill of the prospective driver's license, she'd completely forgotten about a class outline she had to turn in the next day.

She came tearing down the stairs just as I was about to drag myself up them, her eyes as alarmingly wide open as anyone with three-foot lashes can open them, nearly in tears. ''Mom, you've just *got* to help me! I have to turn in an outline tomorrow. Mom, I'm so tired; can't you whip up some ideas for me?'' It so happened my eyes were about as closed as they could be for someone who had only three eyelashes, as it was almost eleven, and I've already impressed you with my early risings so I yawningly inquired as to what lines I should be thinking along. She unblushingly informed me, "Premarital sex." I nearly bit my tongue off bringing that yawn to a screeching halt when I squealed, "*What did you say?*"

She took a look at my face. "Why, I'm against it, silly!" That made me feel a little better, but never having been able to think too creatively on chocolate cake, gooey icing, and mountains of ice cream, I waddled off to bed thinking, "Well now, let's se-e-e-e-z-z-z-zzzzz."

But something awakened me at 2:30 A.M. and this time it wasn't heartburn. I thought to myself, "What *did* she say?" and suddenly I realized I'd be playing the fool if I didn't take this golden opportunity to bring some points vividly to her little inquisitive mind that was enclosed in such a very grown-up-looking body.

As an outline came to me, I ran down to the typewriter and put in six carbon copies (one to pin to her pillow, one for her closet, one to frame in her room, one to tape to the back of the commode, one for her boyfriend, Rick—oh yes, and one for her teacher).

I prayed, "Lord, the content is too important to worry about the decency of my doing her homework"; and so out came six copies of "Why I'm Against Premarital Sex" by Laurie Potterbaum (*as told to her by her mother*, I added mentally).

I kept looking at her all through breakfast, and finally blurted out, "Laurie, you *will* practice what you preach, won't you, dear?" and made some other little motherly comments like "Memorize it!"

But the crowning blow fell when she came home from school and reported, "Mom, you know that outline? I only got C+ on it." I was a bit indignant. "Didn't you tell her your mother wrote a book?"

"No, and I didn't bother to tell her my mother wrote the outline. I think she guessed it by that corny moral-of-the-story bit you stuck at the end: 'a lemon squeezed too many times becomes garbage, so beware—you may have to spend the rest of your life with a lemon.' I think that was the dead giveaway."

Well, I thought, *the first part came from Ann Landers. That teacher wouldn't dare give* her a C+! But I also knew I had no business doing my daughter's homework; so I just looked heavenward and said, "Thanks, Lord—I needed that !"

11

About every hour on the hour Laurie marches into the family room wailing, "Honestly, I haven't anything to wear!"

And grimly, I respond, "Yes, I know," as I think of all the gorgeously attired female adolescents parading around the city—in *my* daughter's clothes.

Whenever she can wheedle me into a shopping spree (which is seldom, as full-length mirrors and I just don't see eye-to-waistline), she often consults me as to what she should buy. She'll hold some dainty little thing up to her and ask, "Should I get this?" I sigh and reply, "Well, I don't think it will go too well with Anne's eyes,and it looks a bit too big for Stacy."

And she just groans.

But I'm grateful that I'm still consulted each morning. Every day she comes into the kitchen and inquires, "Does this look all right?" Once or twice I made the observation that I thought something was too tight, to which she quickly hunched her shoulders all round and groaned, "Mother, really! You're getting absolutely senile!" And off she went, prepared to walk shoulder-hunched all day in her world of peers, rather than admit mother was right.

And mother? She goes off to her rocker, her shawl, her bifocals, and her heating pad—or so Laurie would lead her friends to believe. Actually mother goes off to her typewriter with an intense desire to hit hard at the wrong set of values this age is heaping on our children.

With each "I-haven't-anything-to-wear" I try to instill into my daughter the fact that you *can* wear a few things over again as people seldom notice what you are wearing, that a pleasing personality loaded with cheery attitudes is far more important and noticeable than the latest fashion, that people are generally more concerned with themselves anyhow, and would be hard put to tell the next day what you wore. But somehow and sadly, it falls on deaf ears.

I remember well those days as a teen-ager. How painstakingly I wound little threads of hair into itty-bitty pincurls that the young girls of today find so hysterical. I remember how every blemish on my face was a major crisis demanding plastic surgery. I remember the agony of insecurity that enveloped me when I walked into a room and the myriads of lying spirits ready to ruin your entrance by telling you, "You're ugly. That dress looks dumb. You have ugly spots all over your face. You're really a creep. What did you come for? These kids don't really like you. Your folks are poor. These kids are really sharp, not miserable like you are." And no one ever told me that these same lying spirits were trying to deceive the other ones present, as well as myself. In short, we were a miserable bunch of kids trying to cover up our insecurity with a lot of bravado, and in some cases cigarettes on the sly to make us feel important, secure—like grown-ups. (And isn't that a laugh. Because all they have to do is wait a few years and step into the world of grown-ups, then discover they are still playing the same game only in a different setting. They now have the cocktail lounge for a backdrop instead of the school dance, but the insecurity is still the same.)

You see, no one ever told us each one of us was unique and special, created in the image of God, and so loved of Him that He gave us His only Son to die for us that we might go free, and these bonds of insecurity were only fetters made of loosely knotted lies from the enemy of our souls! No one mentioned God had a plan for our lives, and that He intended we should live abundant lives flowing with vibrancy, excitement, and joy because He lives, and so may we. No one ever told us we could exchange our pitiful estimate of ourselves for His grand and glorious estimate of us. We didn't know that our problem was so severe because we were comparing ourselves with one another instead of looking to Him, the author and finisher of our faith and personality. And if anyone would have dared to tell us, we wouldn't have believed him because of the pressure of the peer group that surrounded us.

And of course, this is where maturity comes in. Oh, not in age so much as in attitude. It is giving up continually thinking of ourselves as the center of the universe (the very one that everyone is so intensely engrossed in—or so we think) and replacing it with a realization that all are precious in the sight of God. It is knowing our very individuality is important to Him, that God doesn't love anyone of us more than He does another, and that He died for all. And we should be willing to serve those for whom He died, in spite of how they are dressed, how they react, and what their outward appearance is.

It is with deep regret that I tell you that I often fall prey to this very thing—being more strongly attracted to the "lovable" ones, and not feeling as keenly the needs of the not-so-lovable ones. May God have mercy on me, and not on me alone but on all the others of us who have been so warped and molded by the blatant blasts of TV, declaring that even our toothpaste will render us sexy, the aging process is to be avoided no matter what the cost, the only really "in" thing today is to be so slim and flat you could hide behind a pole lamp, that by all means your hair must have "body," virginity is outmoded, etc.

Lord, how can I tell our teen-agers that we don't *need all this?*

12

If I told you that Thanksgiving Day lies heavily on me, you'd probably misunderstand and think I wasn't eager to have my family all about me. Actually, I'm only trying to tell you that I just stepped off the scale, and believe me! Thanksgiving Day is lying *heavily* on me.

We really had a grand time on Thanksgiving. My dear mom tottered to the piano (she's 83, but still going strong), thinking she'd play a bit, but at the first tinkle of the keys from those aged but nimble fingers, out came a cornet, trombone (so old and abused that Terry had to grease the stem with Noxema—the only remedy Jan had available in her purse), and a guitar; and of course Jamie came struggling through the hall with his entire drum set. (I realize that this is reading like an episode from the Waltons, but it was more like a junior high dance, what with the aroma of Noxema filling the house and mom's flair for snappy music.)

I was specially thankful this year because my sisters and brothers finally let me fix the turkey. It was the first time in fifteen years they allowed me to bring anything but potato chips to a family gathering. I think the fact that nineteen out of twenty-six people came down with food poisoning after that last turkey had something to do with it. Like I always say, "No matter where I serve my guests, it seems they like my *books* the best."

Well, I'm happy to say the turkey was done to a turn, and the entire meal was delicious. And riotous! I'd hate for Emily Post to ever make her way to one of our clan gatherings! It's almost impossible to eat for laughing. I think that's why I so often wear most of my meals down the front of me.

The table was one shimmering mass of silver, as it was just after our silver wedding anniversary. As people were commenting about how good the food was, one smart aleck popped up with, "Yeah, but how come everything tastes like silver polish?"

My sister, Lauraine, and I tried to keep a running tab as to whose "preparations" were most in demand for second helpings so we could rub it in a bit, and needless to say, she came out way ahead as she is a really tremendous cook. And when they would ask for *her* pie, *her* salads, I would mutter, "Well after all, it isn't just anyone who can write a book." Or, "Betcha' no one ever asked for *your* autograph!"

Yes, that particular Thanksgiving Day is a part of the past now. But every day is a day of thanksgiving for the redeemed of God! And it is *so* necessary for admission into His presence, as the Word tells us to "come before his presence with thanksgiving."

And so, if Thanksgiving Day is past, can Christmas Day be far behind? Alas, and no, it can't be. I wish I could be a bit hypocritical at this point and tell you that I shared your enthusiasm. But, in all honesty, I don't. Oh, I love the cookie-baking, the tree-trimming, all the family fun things that go along with it. But always, about the middle of November I cringe as I watch my little ones sidling up to Grandma and saying, "I want this, oh, buy me that," and I feel a bit helpless as I watch greed being manifested.

Take Christmas cards, for instance. I stopped sending them about fifteen years ago. At that time, I approached Gene and said a bit prosaically, "Let's look at it this way: think of all the mailmen whose load we've made a little lighter this year." So I stopped sending them. Each year, the amount of cards we received decreased by about fifteen. Now, the advent of a Christmas card addressed to us brings the children running in to exclaim, "What is it, mom? What *is* it?"

And each time I determine in my heart that Christmas isn't going to be like it was last year, that we are going to keep it very simple, and I'm not going to let it sap me of my spiritual vitality—about then I get into some situation where simplifying is next to impossible, and being drained emotionally can't be avoided.

And then I ask myself questions like: Why is Christmas synonymous with "booze" for the majority? Why do you feel less spiritual after Christmas than you did before? Why do the children seem disgruntled after the last gift has been opened? Why do we feel compelled to buy things for one another that we don't really need and in some cases don't even want? What does Santa have to do with all this? Why do people send you cards only if you sent them one the year before? Why do you never hear the cheery ring of a "Merry Christmas" anymore? Why is there such a letdown when the decorations have disappeared? Do the same people who celebrate His birth ever think of His death and resurrection (or their own)?

No, I don't really think in terms of "bah humbug!" but in terms of "why?"

13

I once heard of an old country preacher who said his favorite verse was "and it came to pass." When asked why, he chuckled, "Cuz, praise God, it isn't here to stay."

I think I'm having one of those days. Someone dropped a blob of jam on the blanket I just finished making for the new grandbaby coming in May. The car won't start and Larry has the flu. Someone got black grease on the newly shampooed carpeting. And the Christmas tree just simply can't remain there in that corner forever!

And just before I left to go grocery shopping (in a borrowed car), I took a tour through the house and muttered to myself, "If a thief would come in here and ransack while we're gone, we'd never even know he'd been here!"

Now, the obvious way to retain my sanity is to praise the Lord. But can you honestly praise the Lord for these things? (Now, be *honest*!) No, but I can praise Him because the blanket is washable. I can praise Him because I have neighbors who will help in the car situation until Gene gets home. I can praise Him because Larry is much better today than yesterday. I can praise Him because it wasn't grease on the rug after all—just mud. And I can praise Him because I am well and able-bodied, and if I hang a "bubonic plague" sign on the door, I can buy myself a few hours without interruption to get the house straightened. I can praise Him because the kids will help me. I can praise Him for the tranquility He gives in the midst of "tribulation." And I can praise Him because He is greater than any problem I might have, and is even now working to restore peace to my heart.

I remember reading in a book by St. Francis de Sales something to the effect that "our daily trials are like flies: It is not their bite that gets us down, so much as the number of them!"

Well, I can praise God, too, for His heavenly "fly swatter"! We all pitched in, and order now reigns out of confusion. The blanket is washed, the carpet scrubbed, the tree and Larry's temperature are both down, the car had only a frozen gas line and is humming again. But I, too, am glad that it "all came to pass, 'cuz it wasn't here to stay!"

14

If you don't listen with an open heart to what I'm about to say, you may easily misunderstand. I think I'm about to hit hard at some traditions and some wrong ways of thinking that we as Americans have picked up.

Somehow, the Spirit of God is making me very aware of people's words. And as I listen, I find that we rob ourselves of much joy because we do things from wrong motives. More and more I'm realizing that this walk with the Lord is primarily concerned with our reactions to circumstances and our motives for doing what we do.

I'm hearing things like this. "I don't mind doing something for someone when they appreciate it."

"After I went to all that trouble, do you know that she never even noticed?"

"Well, you'd think she could have at least sent a thank you card!"

"I'm tired of being a sweet, docile wife. I've tried it for two weeks, and he hasn't even noticed."

I could go on and on, but the basic point I'm trying to get across is our age-old proneness to "giving, providing I will get something back in return." But the Word of God makes it very clear that God wants us to "do whatsoever we do, heartily, as *unto the Lord*." Then, our "thank you's," our appreciation, would flow from His heart into ours, and we would learn the valuable lesson that comes when we discover that what is done in secret is still the most pleasing to Him. The very moment we desire any human response, our heavenly response from Him is shut off to a certain extent.

Oh, I know that we as Christians should be the first to send thank-you notes and we should be the first to express appreciation.

But I also know that as Christians, we should be the first *not* to expect thanks, nor to look for words of appreciation. If we could just learn to do all as "unto the Lord," we would be so pleased about having pleased Him, we would no longer be looking for any crumbs of thanks the world might have to offer.

And when a thank you is extended, nine chances out of ten we become judgmental if the thanks didn't have the degree of warmth we thought it should have had.

We'll go out of our way to say things like "she told me she liked it, but I don't think she really did." (I am most guilty of this, because I always have this uneasy feeling that people are not going to like what I've picked out for them. But that's prejudging also.) And then there are comments like my married son, Don, makes when I've picked out a shirt for him: "Mom, I really like this. I can wear it with a vest, a sports jacket, and a muffler, and it will hardly show. Yeah, mom. This will be fine."

And phone calls that say, "Mom, where did you say you bought this? It's—uh, you know—too big."

Or maybe it's Laurie, sailing out the door the day after Christmas with her arms loaded with packages to return. "You don't mind, do you, mom?"

And no, I don't mind. These crazy kids have found that we have a lot more fun if we poke fun at one another, and I have a sneaky suspicion that in the gift-buying department I do fall a little short. (The cat even rejected the flea collar I bought him by wriggling out of it at every turn!)

Well, what does it matter? I don't mind their rejecting my gifts so long as they don't reject *me!*

"*You don't mind, do you, mom?*"

15

Are you hungry for a blessing? Need a little lift in your day? Would you like to have a "close-in" view of a husband loving his wife as "Christ loved the church"? Then settle back and enjoy this letter I received after returning from a speaking engagement in Aurora, Illinois.

Dear Char:

Praise the name of our Lord Jesus! Just wanted to tell you thanks again for being at our first AGLOW meeting. You can say you launched AGLOW in Aurora. I truly enjoyed having you. I am sorry about the problem with the microphone but our Father allowed it for a reason and I believe it was for that man who was called in to work on it. He became very interested in what you were saying. Did you notice that he didn't leave the room? He went to the back and stood. After the meeting he told a lady that he had never heard such singing like that in all his life and did we do it all the time? So some seeds have been planted within him and for this I praise God. It was all worth it for one soul.

I would have loved to have taken you aside and just shared with you for hours. I witnessed within you that same hunger for more and more and more of Jesus. I couldn't be selfish though, as I know there were many others who wanted to share with you, too. It was reported that what you said about submission touched one girl who was about to leave her husband that same day. After hearing you speak she changed her mind. Praise God that He worked through you.

Oh, how this message about submission is needed for the women—and for it to be taught in the right way. So many people say "do this" and "do that" and you are in submission. God has shown me that submission is not something you do. It is a state of being, a heart thing. You can't work your way into submission any more than you can work your way to heaven. The best way to learn submission is to learn of Jesus. He is our submission. You know where it says in the Bible that the older women are to teach the younger how to love their husbands? People take that and tear it apart when it is so simple. In order to teach them how to love their husbands, teach them about Jesus. It is only with His love that we can love them in the right way. So many women wear themselves out doing *so many things* for their husbands because they are taught that this is submission, when really their heart is not in the doing.

I have found that when the attitude of the heart is right, all these *things* just seem to follow. You do them for your husband and children because you love them through the Lord. It all centers around Jesus. I've heard it said that all homes center around the mother. This is the problem today in America. They have centered around the woman instead of around Jesus. If the women could turn it over to the Lord they would all be in fine shape. Amen??

This is one lesson the Lord had to teach me right away. You see, *my husband and I have been married to each other three times and I was married to two others in between*. So I have been the rounds in marriage. Char, my husband had the fruit of the Spirit through all of that. So much love and patience with me. Would you believe he never married anyone else, but took me back with open arms *every time* I wanted to come back—and then without a word? Just like our Father always accepts us back when we break fellowship with Him.

Charles (my husband) never knew when he came home from work whether he was going to find me or a note waiting for him. I don't know how he got through those years without having a nervous breakdown because my life was an endless search for something, yet he was the one who had to suffer. He has never to this day brought up anything that I did! He is really an unbelievable person. I thank God for him. One day I came to the end of myself after years and years of hell. I was so sick of *me*! I was actually physically sick. I had a twenty-four-hour-a-day hurt in my side and back. I had two surgeries with no improvement.

I was not completely godless all those years. I would remember every so often that I walked up an aisle in a Baptist church when I was younger and said, "I accept Jesus as my Savior." I may have said it but there was no change in my life to prove it. I am so thankful that God doesn't give up on us. One day I just couldn't cope any longer. I went to my bedroom and I cried unto God these words: "God, I am so tired of trying to live this life, won't you please take me and make me what you want me to be?" That was the end of *me*, Char. God welcomed me back just as He does every prodigal. From that day on the Lord began to work on me, and in me. I went to church every now and then during those sick years (about two). Maybe I went to church three or four times at the most. Anyway, I suppose to try and draw me in they asked me if I would be a teacher's helper. Me! Someone who didn't know anything but John 3:16 and didn't really know what *that* meant. But I told them I would, whenever I was able to make it to church.

The very first time I helped, wouldn't you know! The woman they put me with had received the baptism in the Holy Spirit. She asked me if I believed in this experience. I said "Yes, I guess so." You see, I was so ignorant I didn't even know what she was talking about, but I didn't want her to know that. She asked if I would like to go to a Bible study. I said yes. I didn't go, though, not for weeks. I found out later that she just kept praying for me. Finally one day I went (during this time I had been trying to understand the Bible and was drawing closer to God.) I felt a certain excitement at that Bible study and saw something different. I knew they had something I didn't have. I just seemed to blend right in with them from that very first day.

One thing got me, though. They talked about women being in submission to their husbands. I wondered about that, but they were in the Word so who could argue? The next time I went they got into the baptism in the Holy Spirit. I really didn't understand anything about it, but I stayed later that day, listening. Then, as I was driving home by myself, I said a simple prayer: "Lord, if what they have is from you, I want it.''

The Holy Spirit just fell on me. The light of the Lord came on within me and seemed to be throughout the car! Oh, Char, He even spoke to me and said, ''It is faith, Janice, it is faith.'' I felt like I had stepped out of darkness into light, or maybe like a person would feel after being asleep for years and had awakened and the world had become a beautiful, wonderful place.

Well, needless to say, I was transformed inside and out. My sickness began to go away. The Holy Spirit began regaining the ground Satan (and Janice) had taken.

Our children were saved and Charles came back to the Lord. (I don't really think he ever left Him, in his heart—he just didn't go to church.) And we both know that this whole thing is not *church*. It is *heart*. Right? Now of course, you know I am with AGLOW and Charles and I have children's worship at our church. Charles has not received the baptism as yet, but he says he has surrendered his life to God. So I know that since he is willing, he will eventually receive all that God has for him. I think it is hard for those who have always had such good morals to realize they need this power released in them. He had to suffer because of me, but was not literally dragged through the gutter as I was. Can you believe that I praise the Lord for all those problems now? They have all worked out for my good. I hope it doesn't sound pious, but ''she who has been forgiven much, loves much,'' and that is how I feel. Sometimes all I can say is ''Lord, Lord'' when His presence is so real.

I must go now. I love you in Jesus,

Janice S.

16

When the end of the month rolls around, most people think of their bills. Not me. I know by the calendar that the time has come for me to reach the end of Proverbs (a chapter a day keeps the blahs away). And once again I must say, "Mirror, mirror of the Word—the virtuous woman, she is preferred."

I draw some comfort from the fact that even the Holy Spirit is willing to admit that the woman of Proverbs 31 is a rare jewel: "A capable, intelligent, and virtuous woman, who is he who can find her?" (Amplified) Well, *he'd* be one exhausted fellow, he would, if he tried to find her. He'd be far better to marry the one God has chosen for him, then stand back and give God lots of elbow room to change her! If he loves her as Christ loved the church, she will blossom and burst into something that is comparable to the precious jewels mentioned.

In verse 11 (of Proverbs 31), we find that "the heart of her husband trusts in her confidently," . . . so that he has no lack of honest gain" (she will not stand in his way as I did when Gene wanted to work to prosper his business) "or need of dishonest spoil." (I know of one wife who complained so much that because her husband didn't earn enough to buy the things she wanted, he resorted to dishonest means to please his wife. He permitted her demands to sway him from honest beliefs, thereby making her an idol.)

Verse 12 says, "She will comfort, encourage, and do him *only* good as long as there is life within her." Lord, that one hurts. I have not always done him good; I have not always encouraged him. Couldn't we change the subject, Lord?

Verse 13: "She seeks out the wool and flax and works with willing hands to develop it." (Sometimes I frown at sewing on a button.)

Verse 14: "She is like the merchant ships loaded with foodstuffs." Well, I've never heard my matronly figure compared to a tanker, but . . . I sure have loaded this matronly figure with foodstuffs in times past (and now I'm wondering if I ever should have started this chapter!)

Verse 15: At last, one I can revel in: "She rises while yet it is night and gets spiritual food for her household and assigns her maids their tasks." By nature, I've always been a late riser. But with spiritual growth come disciplines. Disciplines would not be disciplines if they didn't cut against the very grain of your nature. So, and as I've mentioned, due to a slow metabolism that needs the two-hour start on my family plus the desire to follow the Lord's example, I started rising at 5:00. And what a joy it has been. Granted, there are a few mornings that I goof off, but I know I have lost a blessing that God would have granted if I hadn't catered to the flesh. I heartily recommend this discipline, but only in God's timing. I've learned from experience that He disciplines gently, not putting too many on you at one time, easing you from one discipline into another almost without your knowing it.

And once, while mulling verse 15 over in my mulling-over-place, I asked, "Lord, How can I assign my maids their tasks? I don't have any. Maids, I mean. Tasks, I have." I couldn't be quite satisfied with thinking this meant pushing an assortment of buttons at the right times, so, while I was doing dishes, He answered me. Quietly, He said, "your attitudes." What a blessing that was! Right attitudes would lessen our work strain!

I could see what He meant. Early each day, we should spend some time with Him so that our attitudes could become *His* attitudes. Each one should be lined up within us so that they are under the control of the Spirit instead of our allowing our attitudes and emotions to control us. (This would be the same as "keeping our hearts with all diligence, for out of it are the issues of life.")

I'm glad I feel at home in verse 15, because I get all squirmy when we move into verse 16. "She considers a new field before she buys or accepts it—expanding prudently." Obviously, this virtuous woman has a business head about her. Me? See Gene. He'd remember the time when I was filling out a credit application for an elderly couple. I read off, "Name? Address? Telephone? Marital status?" Then I leaned compassionately over the counter and inquired, "Tell me, are you happily married?" I think that's when he and Don put me back to bathroom-scrubbing in a hurry!

But I think I am a bell ringer when it comes to the next part: "and not courting neglect of her present duties by assuming others." I'm a firm believer in saying no when I see that we are not taking the time to be a family. We'll even say no to important meetings, rather than have the kids be unhappy, even the older ones. They need us too.

Then, we read that "with her savings [of time and strength] she plants fruitful vines in her vineyard." To me, that says that right attitudes mean renewed vigor and renewed vigor means additional strength to sow the seeds of righteousness. These seeds of righteousness (or right ways of living) mean fruitful vines and vines are things that cling. So I have the responsibility of teaching my children, plus all the dear ones the Lord sends our way, that Christ is the true Vine, and we must cling to Him tenaciously in utter dependence, for without Him we can do nothing!

I have to limp a bit in verse 17. "She girds herself with strength [spiritual, mental and physical fitness for her God-given task] and makes her arms strong and firm." Well, nobody's perfect. Oh, I think I do all right with the spiritual, due to an insatiable hunger for the Word of God. But as for the mental, I really don't knock myself out keeping abreast of secular things. And the physical? What would you expect from the girl who was always left standing in the middle of the gym floor when sides were being chosen, trying not to hear them argue, "*you* take her. . . . No, we had her last time. *You* take her."

Consequently, because I didn't make my muscles work for me in my youth, I have a measure of stamina, and that is all. A measure. Arms strong and firm? The only thing strong and firm about me is my convictions! I "gird" the rest of me.

Verse 18 is to my liking also. "She tastes and sees that her gain from work [with and for God] is good; her lamp goes not out; but it burns on continually through the night [of trouble, privation or sorrow, warning away fear, doubt, and distrust]." Though we have not had much sorrow or privation, still this "lamp" has been used many times to burn out fear when others unknowingly have tried to make their fears become a part of me; and this lamp has been most useful in burning out mistrust.

I guess we'd have to give a spiritual application to verse 19, because in all honesty, I have never put my hands to the spindle or the distaff. I'm not even sure what they are! But it sounds like something to do with weaving. Haven't we as wives played a tremendous role in weaving and shaping the lives of these children He has placed in our hands? And who but Almighty God could untangle the threads when we mess up our "sampler"?

Verse 20 will humble you in a jiffy. Have you always opened your hand to the poor? I haven't *always*. And my hands have not *always* been filled to reach out to the "needy [whether in body, mind or spirit]." For far too long my hands were filled with me—my problems, my concerns. Praise God, there is always hope for the future.

Oh, I really like verse 21. "She fears not the snow for her family, for all her household are *doubly* clothed in scarlet. "Doubly"—to me that speaks only not of salvation but the baptism in the Holy Spirit as well!

We read on that "she makes herself coverlets, cushions and rugs of tapestry." I like that, too. It gives me comfort for it makes me think God understands this woman's heart of mine that likes to have her home comfortable. (I think even if God called me to darkest Africa I would still require a lace doily and a candlestick holder! And maybe a potted palm.)

In verse 23, we find her husband sitting with the elders at the city gates. And somehow, it didn't disturb our virtuous woman. You and I would have been furious. We would have accused him of loving his business better than he did us.

And here she is in verse 24, using that business head again. She "makes fine linen garments and leads others to buy them." Sounds persuasive, doesn't she? "She delivers to the merchants girdles [for sashes that free one for service]." She was just generally being a blessing to everyone. Yet, she still had time to run her house, communicate with her children, help her neighbors, and dabble a bit in real estate and business on the side!

I can only say "mirror, mirror of the Word—any comparison would be absurd!"

17

Father, it's New Year's Day! We have just touched our toe into the icy waters of the new year. The water is cold, Lord, but we will get used to it. And who knows? Perhaps You will part the waters, and we will go forth on dry ground.

Yes, the waters seem as cold as death. Maybe because death has touched us on two points, this first day of the year. For Frostie went home to be with You just two days ago.

Frostie was a dear Catholic sister in Christ who loved Him with a tenderness that warmed my heart. After she had read my first book, she'd expressed a desire to meet me. (It's amazing how curious people get about a woman who accidentally caused her hubby to get his bedrooms mixed up!)

Now mind you, I went to Frostie, chin up and bravely, because I thought I had a real task on my hands. I, mighty counselor of women, was on my way to cheer up a saint who was looking death in the face because of the dreaded enemy, cancer.

She told her friend, Nancy, "Let's meet her in a restaurant some place. You know how I love my cats, and she might not understand—so much cat hair and all. You know I try, but my cats are all I have." She made this statement after she had read the first few chapters of *If You See Lennie*.

But after she'd finished the book, she said, "Nance, just bring her here. Somehow, I don't think she'll mind at all." No doubt it was the bit about the piles of laundry or maybe sending the ironing to the Good Will store so I could buy it back all mended and ironed.

So Nancy made the arrangements, picked me up, and took me off to what turned out to be one of the sweetest experiences of my life.

The first delight came when we pulled up to a small cottage-type home that was white, trimmed in loving care and pink. Flowers, shrubs, trellises and enchantment, all rolled into one corner lot.

And then we stepped into the "play house" and couldn't help but "oo" and "ah" at its charm. A tiny maiden lady who went by the wacky name of Frostie met us at the door. Her name was certainly a misnomer for she was all warmth and humor, and we knew the moment our eyes met that we were friends forever. She carefully pointed out to us that she put her beloved "animals" in the back bedroom, and hoped we didn't mind if we found a cat hair or two around. (The house was spotless and shimmering, but I delighted her by dramatically picking imaginary hairs out of the air and out of my mouth as we chatted.)

What did we talk about? We talked about her homegoing! She was absolutely excited about thinking that she might be with her Lord even before Christmas (the doctors had given her until November).

With eyes shining, she said, "Oh, I've so much to get done. I hope to get my shopping finished. Stocker will do it for me. And then, I have so many last things to tie up before I go. My, I can hardly wait. I've read every book I can get my hands on about heaven, plus all the Scriptures. Oh, it's going to be so grand! I guess my only concern is the pain that will increase. But when I think of how He suffered for us, it seems like a very small thing. You see, I'm really so undecided, I know He can heal me, but what if it is my ordained time for departure? I long so to be with Him. I have no husband, no family. Stocker will take my animals and love them as much as I have. No, I'm just not sure.

"And yet, there are so many people where I used to work who would be touched by a miraculous healing. But that's another thing. If I'm healed, I would have to go back to work!"

We laughed uproariously. She was such a delight. I suppose the hardest thing to understand was the fact that she looked the picture of health! More like a radiant bride about to meet her bridegroom who'd been gone for a long time.

As we began to talk about the will of God, we began to itemize why it would be good if she could remain here among the living. Then we began to talk about the advantages of going home to be with the Lord (and believe me, the reasons for departing far outweighed the advantages of staying!).

And so, we departed on this happy note: the best way to have God's will for your life is to have no will of your own!

Well, it was an exciting visit, and more so because Frostie was going off to a Kathryn Kuhlman meeting that next weekend. We didn't know what God had in store for her, but we knew that she had an openness toward His will for she had put her future entirely into His hands.

But, as God would have it, Frostie happened to see Kathryn Kuhlman on a television show just prior to her going. (A note on Miss Kuhlman: I have been to one of her miracle meetings. I have seen the power of God at work. I have seen with my own eyes how mightily God used her as an instrument through which He could work. Immediately I realized why Satan does all he can to "turn people off" to her as a person. He even worked on me as I sat in her meeting. At first, I was offended by her dramatic showmanship. How dared such a slip of a woman direct that choir with such a flair when she was supposed to be "in the background"? But God was patient with me. It was as though He said, "Just wait. You'll see." And then it happened. She began to speak. Suddenly, I was only aware of God—my love for Him, His love for me—by His Spirit He spoke to me through her, His trusted instrument. It wasn't that her words were so profound. It was the keen awareness of the love relationship she had developed with this Jesus. And quietly, lovingly, He began to answer openly the cry of her heart that He had heard in the secret place as miracles began happening all around us. She had the right to be as dramatic and "showy" as her heart desired. When I have done more for the Lord than she has, then I will have the right to criticize her method of doing it!)

Frostie was "turned off"! She called me, and was most upset. She said, "I don't think I like her. She talks spooky. I'm not even sure I want to go to the meeting."

I laughed. "Frostie, she is used to speaking before huge audiences. She has to speak in a most pronounced way. And I understand that at one time she had a speech impediment. She has overcome it completely, but still must measure each word carefully."

"Oh."

"Also, let me mention one other thing. Wait a minute, I'll get my Bible. Here, let me read this to you. In Isaiah, it says—no, wait. I want my Living Bible."

She laughingly said, "Hey, will you make up your mind? I don't have *too* many minutes left, you know!" And how I praised God for her delightful humor.

I came back to the phone and read this passage from Isaiah 53, a reference to Christ: "In God's eyes he was like a tender green shoot, sprouting from a root in dry and sterile ground. But in our eyes there was no attractiveness at all, nothing to make us want him. We despised him and rejected him—a man of sorrows, acquainted with bitterest grief. We turned our backs on him and looked the other way when he went by. He was despised and we didn't care."

"Frostie, it isn't the comeliness of a person that should ever attract us. It should be the inner man, the spirit of the person that appeals to us. Go to her meeting, Frostie. You will be so pleased. Take my word for it. If I had never been there, I would not be so sure of my words. But when this little woman begins to speak to God, and then to the people—something happens! And it can't be of the Enemy as so many would like to make you think because you will be so much more in love with Christ when you leave that place. And I can't see that that has ever been the aim of the devil at any time!"

She thanked me, agreeing that we make a mistake when we start looking at the outward appearance of people, a most human reaction to say the least. And she did go to the meeting, and God did not heal her, but she was so blessed! She said it was an even greater preparation for her departure from this life. She said she saw miracles happening all around her.

And so, quietly, as the prayer group prayed the New Year in last night, we thanked God for welcoming Frostie into His presence, and thanked Him for giving her to us as an example of glowing anticipation as she prepared for her "transfer."

The Word tells us that "precious in the sight of the Lord is the death of his saints." How can we think of it as anything but precious to us? And these are the words I must speak tomorrow as I go to comfort Katie.

Katie is a tiny woman not much bigger than the broken reed spoken of in the Word. But tomorrow, she will be showing forth the greatness of the Comforter as she stands beside the casket of her little Karen, who was only twelve when God called her home. Katie, her husband, and two of her six daughters were vacationing in Mexico. A happy time, to be sure. But a "faulty furnace" in a Mexican motel snuffed out the life of this precious little one. And when I heard it, my first immediate reaction was "God, how could You! What tragedy! What waste!" And so patiently, He waited for the supernatural reaction He'd wanted in the first place.

He said, "Truly, I am the blessed controller of all things. Haven't you yourself told others that? Her parents trusted Me with her care. I make no mistakes. Don't look on this the way the world does, as tragic and careless waste. See it through My eyes; help Katie to praise Me for having had Karen for twelve years and help others realize that death is a part of life, a part of reality, that there should be no boasting about tomorrow, for no one knows what a day might bring forth. Do you, My people, My creation, have any right to tell Me, the Potter, what I should do with My created ones? Please be still in My hands. I know what I am doing. Rest quietly here, until your feathers become unruffled. Then fly quietly, harmlessly as a dove, to Katie tomorrow, and bring My peace to her, as others are being told to do."

Yes, Lord. The waters are icy cold this New Year's Day. And one can't help but know this old earth is creaking and groaning on its axis. The Bible tells us that "Thou Lord, in the beginning hast laid the foundation of the earth, and the heavens are the work of thy hands: They shall perish, but thou continuest; and they all shall wax old as doth a garment; and as a mantle shalt thou roll them up, as a garment, and they shall all be changed: But thou are the same, and thy years shall not fail" (Heb. 1:11-12 Phillips).

Father, like a soiled pinafore we are spread out before You. Our ruffles are tattered by pollution, pockets are torn by political clashes. We've tried so hard to patch and tidy our garment, but see? Truly we have "waxed old like a garment." Yet, our times are in Your hands, O Lord. There would be no hope for the future apart from You and the promises You've given to us in Your Word. Your Word has become a lamp to our feet, Lord. As You lead the way, we can know that we are safe. Amen

18

Now I know why they stoned the prophets—because the truth they preached touched sore spots, causing something to ooze forth that triggered intense reactions. Twice this week I've come close to being slugged by two irate wives. It happened like this:

Gene and I were on the summer porch. Neither of us jumped up when the doorbell rang, as we thought it was the usual ding-dong of a neighborhood small fry. So we were a bit startled when Mark ushered in a young mother, obviously upset. I immediately sensed we were in for a real dandy. I was so glad Gene was there, for I knew he'd step in and temper my words if I got out of my element.

Marty started the conversation by saying, "I can't go on, I just can't. Since Skip has left, the kids are uncontrollable. Everything is going to pieces at home, including me. He isn't paying the bills. I simply can't go on!" And she started to cry.

I said firmly, "That isn't true! You *can* go on, and what's more, you *must* go on. Don't even give yourself one more moment to believe that you *can't* go on. Others have done it before you, and others will do it after you. This is not the end of the world."

I knew she was having a tough time, but sympathy was the last thing she needed at this point. But we also knew she needed to release some of the emotion she was struggling with.

Defiantly, she said, "But others don't have three small kids to think about, no car, and no job. What am I supposed to do?" And she proceeded to spew out some venom against her estranged mate who had left because pressures were too great. We let her get it out of her system. Gene's learned enough about women to know that occasionally they need to give vent to their emotional pressures.

Gently—oh, I do so hope it was gently—we began to probe and say the things we felt the Holy Spirit would have us say. Things that took supernatural strength to say, and buckets of grace to receive.

We told her that there could be no hope of reconciliation until she was willing to go to her husband and take all the blame on herself. Oh, how galling to the flesh these words of counsel are, how everything rises up within one's soul in defense. Yet, here is where the deathblow is dealt—in the willingness of a soul to accept all the blame for a situation that has arisen.

She jumped up, crying uncontrollably now, and was ready to stalk off the summer porch when I said, "Marty, don't leave like this. Let's pray. We want to help you see the value of going this route."

Reluctantly, she came back and sat down. We prayed with her and asked God for wisdom, asking Him to help her see the reality of what we were so haltingly trying to say.

Gene said, "Marty, it's like this. When you stand in the place of blame, absorbing it all, it doesn't leave any blame for the other person. There is no finger of accusation you can point at them. But when you are accusing him of even a small percentage of blame, you are drying up the channels of healing that should flow."

Marty cried, "You'll have to prove that from Scripture before I can accept it! He's not taking care of us . . . He's *worse* than an infidel! The Bible says so!"

We did our best to make her see that we realized there are always two sides to any story, but that God's principles work, and her willingness to absorb all the blame would make way for a reconciliation. Long ago we discovered that there must be one of the two who is willing to take the whole brunt of the pain, in order for healing to come through.

Well, at least she calmed down after we prayed instead of walking out in a huff. But I was a bit stymied when she challenged, "Prove it to me from Scripture" because I myself had always told her to check everything out with the Word of God before she accepted it as gospel truth. So I decided I'd better do some searching myself.

I really couldn't think of chapter and verse that would back this up, but I knew it was a basic principle. When she said this, the only thing I could come up with was the fact that Christ was our example, and had done exactly this when He died for our sins—the innocent dying for the guilty! He had taken all our sins on Himself, though He was guiltless, that we might go free! And then He prayed, "Father, forgive them, they know not what they do."

Weakly, she said, "But I'm not God! And I'm not ready to see this line of reasoning yet. You'll have to give me some time."

And we realized she'd need time, as every untended thing around the house, every unpaid bill, every neglected need was in her eyes a shining testimonial to her husband's outrageous indifference to her and the children's needs. And, humanly, we had to agree that she had every natural reason to be upset and angry; but we also agreed that we serve a God who wants us to do the *supernatural!*

Gene assured her that God wouldn't let her starve to death, nor would the church, nor would we. We helped her to recall why she still had reason to praise God, and encouraged her to take stock of her own heart's attitudes, for out of her heart are the "issues of life." Gene made her see that the bitterness and resentment she was allowing to build up would only cause poison to seep into her own system, for vengeance belongs unto the Lord and He is the only one who can deal properly with His children. Our emotional and physical bodies can't take the strain. They "break down" somewhere.

A few days after she left, I was reading in Colossians and came across this in the Living Bible: "He forgave all your sins, and blotted out the charges proved against you, the list of his commandments which you had not obeyed. He took this list of sins and destroyed it by nailing it to Christ's cross. In this way God took away Satan's power to accuse you of sin, and God openly displayed to the whole world Christ's triumph at the cross where your sins were all taken away" (2:13-15).

As I mused the passage over, these thoughts came to my mind: Taking all the blame would be following Christ's example, but to point a finger of blame would be following Satan's example; we'd

80

be taking away Satan's power to accuse when we openly say, "I am to blame"; then we in turn could put that blame on the cross where Jesus bore it all for us anyhow! As all blame was already nailed to the cross, we could take the blame and quickly put it on to Christ who willingly bore it all for us. Oh, do you follow me? If my blame was nailed there, isn't the blame that belongs to the other placed there also? Then, if blame has been dealt with, wouldn't it be possible to make a new start? But not until God had worked this all thoroughly into our individual hearts.

Well, Marty is still struggling with this. But I believe her love for Christ is sincere, and He will reveal the truth to her. Indeed, He is the only one who can.

That same day, another mother came our way. She was about to split from her fifth, yes, *fifth* husband. She very coolly told me that they were getting a divorce because they "couldn't get along." I don't know what she expected from me. I merely gave her a very weak, "Oh? I see." Divorce had become such an easy out to her—who was I to tamper with such a simple solution? But I did.

I let her have all the room she needed in the conversation, then interrupted her when I'd had all I could take. She said, "Well, we just don't get along." And I said, "But you could if you'd ever come to realize that love is giving, not getting." I'm sure I said it without rancor. But it was too much.

She got up, walked toward the door, turned to me, and said, "Do me a favor—don't use me in your book."

I promised, "I won't," and I haven't. Other than this conversation, you'll never know her story.

But there are the happy endings. Like the time Lee called. Lee is in her second marriage and has only recently come to Christ. Her husband hasn't. The other morning about 7:00 I got a call from Lee. I stumbled to the phone, having treated myself to a late rising that day, only to hear her saying—with great control—"Char, what should I do? I just found Ray with another woman."

Obviously, there is no end to the heartbreak we have all around us.

I thought a moment, then I said, "Do you love him?"
"Yes."
"Then forgive him. Can you do that?"

She was quiet for a moment, then said, "Yes, I think I can." I talked to her a bit longer about weighing this injury against the tremendous possibility of Ray's being in eternity with the Lord someday, when she would finally realize it was worth it all, and as raunchy as his offense was in our sight, still *his worse offense in the sight of God was Christ-rejection*; we needed to see this as his prime offense with all others seeming small in comparison to it. We talked about the Scripture that says God is well pleased when we suffer for His sake. Then I ended the conversation, went back and curled up beside my sleepy, faithful, eyes-for-no-one-but-me husband and patted his unshaven face, thanking God from the bottom of my heart for this good man who has endured so much from me, uncomplainingly. After a conversation like the one I just took part in, his faults seemed very small. It wasn't at all difficult to focus on his good points and to praise God for giving him to me. I was more than happy to cook his breakfast that morning. And I couldn't help thinking, "Thanks, Lord—I needed that!"

19

We were winding our way around a mountainous road. Gene was driving and the boys were asleep in the back seat. Gene seemed to be absorbed in his own thoughts so we just rode along, allowing the silence to be most companionable.

Suddenly I started to giggle. Gene is used to this, but his curiosity always wins out. So he said, ''What's so funny?'' And by then I was laughing so hysterically I could hardly bring myself to tell him. With what measure of sobriety I could muster, I pointed to two small trails of smoke curling up through the trees on the mountainside.

Now, I know that doesn't sound hilarious in itself, but it all had to do with a firefighter who was flying about, making himself quite available to put out any least bit of fire he might spot.

Gene said, ''I don't get it. Why should that be such a scream?'' Holding my sides, I explained what I thought anyone would assume. ''Can't you just picture those two Indians down there? One has gotten his little pile of wood together and just started out with his message after rubbing his two sticks together. He says, 'Dear Brother Ringworm, could you—and 'fh-t-t-t-t!' along comes the firefighter and wipes out his message. And Brother Ringworm on the other side of the mountain answers back, 'Could I wh—' and the firefighter dashes over there.'' By now the boys were up and giggling.

Gene just kind of shook his head in a knowing sort of way.

But it all caused me to be grateful for my sense of humor, a truly magnificent gift from the Lord! And it also caused me to be grateful that I lived in a country that had firefighters instead of people fighters dashing about in the sky.

Seeing the tall towers where the firefighters watched over the forests reminded me of our jaunt behind the Iron Curtain. A few years ago, Gene had won us trips to Austria through his business, and one of the side trips available was a "day" behind the Iron Curtain, taking us across the border into Bratislava, Czechoslavakia.

We had all gotten merrily into our bus in beautiful, carefree Austria, thinking this would just be another outing. Little did we know how depressed we would be by what we were going to see. When the bus pulled up to the border, we were struck by the fact that the Russian guards had taken time to plant flowers that were quite cheerful. But after they had checked our papers and we made our way across "no-man's land," we were suddenly gripped by the immensity of the danger.

Innocent pheasants were walking saucily through the mined fields of "no-man's land," oblivious to the fact that the heaviness of a man's foot would send both man and gorgeous pheasant into eternity. Guards watched us carefully from their towers; and as the guide pointed out, there were two guards—one to watch the border and one to watch the other guard. He also pointed out the fact that no Austrian cared to enter, so of course they were trying to keep the Czechs "in."

As we came into Bratislava, the first thing we noticed was the absence of cars. Here we were in a city of around 250,000 people and hardly a car in sight. It was specially disturbing when you came into the center of town because in our country the traffic noise drowns out the sound of thousands of pairs of shuffling feet. But as we got out of our bus, all we could hear were those feet—shuffling feet of somber people who eyed us suspiciously without the least hint of a smile.

Our tour guide was quite a sight in himself. He was bigger around than he was tall and had given us strict warning to go only where he went—which posed quite a problem for me when he made his way into the men's room because I was clinging to his robust coattail every moment of the tour. Gene quickly made it clear to me that I couldn't follow him there, but how could I know that, not being able to read the signs over the doors?

And when I finally realized we would be safe for the few moments we'd be in the ladies' room, I made my way there, only to be deflated when the washroom attendant refused the American coins I dropped into her dish. (I didn't realize that having those American coins in her possession could have landed her in prison until I read some books by the Wurmbrands.)

Franz, our guide, gathered us together in the hotel lobby, then ushered us into the hotel tearoom. The waitress who served us reeked with a terrible body odor, so unbearable that we could hardly stand it; but our guide had already prepared us having mentioned earlier that we must realize that some things Americans consider necessities (such as soap and deodorant) are considered luxuries to these people. He had also explained to us that even though the clerks would look fairly well dressed, these clothes were worn just like uniforms. They were provided by the State but had to be hung up in back rooms until the next working day.

The stores were quite dismal, for they have no incentive to make one store more attractive than another to encourage eye appeal to the shopper. If you wanted an item and you didn't buy it in their store, you would just walk down to the next store and buy the same thing there for the same price. They didn't really care where you bought because everything was owned by the State anyhow, and all their salaries were the same—small.

When we stepped into the street, we noticed that the stores bore names (in Czech, of course) that simply stated "Shoes," "Dresses," "Hats," "Purses." There were no cheery neon lights beckoning you to come in and shop and price and pick and choose. It was all very dull and monotonous.

We saw buildings propped up by telephone poles that had been stuck into gaping holes in the pavement. We saw naked gypsy children running about. We saw streets being flushed due to the custom of relieving oneself at curb-stands. The depression these people were under numbed us, and caused us to look forward to going back hastily to fresh, crisp Austria!

While at a different hotel for an evening meal, we ate a meat that had a most unusual flavor, highly spiced. Later we were told that dog meat is quite a delicacy in Bratislava, and to this day we are wondering!

It was with gratitude that we made our way back to our buses. As we pulled away from the city, we turned around, only to see that huge city plunged into darkness, not one light of cheer, only stark loneliness staring back.

At the border again, we were asked to get out of the bus. We watched as the guards took their flashlights and got down on their knees to inspect the underneath carriage of the bus to be sure that no determined Czech had decided to enter Austria with us. It was a most eerie experience, and how we cheered as we got through the border back into gentle Austria. Faintly, from the front of the bus we could hear the strains of "Edelweiss," and then a rousing round of "The Star-Spangled Banner" joined in by all!

Yes, I'm so glad I live in America. Does it hurt you deep inside when you hear people complain about our government? It does me, too—specially having seen this other government close up. It would do us good to remember how displeased the Lord was with those who murmured and complained in the wilderness. I know there is corruption but that stems from the hearts of men. It would do us well to thank God frequently that we live in this free country and that we do lead a life that's "quiet and peaceable."

Thank you, Jesus, for Your goodness to us.

20

We had just returned from Gettysburg. We'd been gone almost a week, so of course there was much to do in the house, and I'd gotten a bit behind on my correspondence. I knew the kids were playing in the back yard and was delighted because there hadn't been any neighborhood scraps or complaining whatsoever. I thought, "No doubt Mark and Jamie are telling them all about Gettysburg," as I heard sounds that were supposed to be cannons, war whoops, and so on.

During a coffee break, I stepped to the picture window that faces our back yard. What a scene I beheld. Let me picture it for you.

Mark had found some old telephone wire spools. To these, he'd mounted some pieces of vent-pipe. All of this was tied neatly together with something—wait, let me look a bit closer. Good grief! Yes, it is. My old pantyhose are holding all that together! To this, they'd nailed a piece of inner tubing, resulting in a giant sling shot to maneuver green apples through the cannon for the North, and buckeyes through the "shoot" for the South! As missiles were flying back and forth, I heard something that sounded like a real cannon in the distance. They had found how to tape three cans together, and with just the right touch of a match to some lighter fluid in the bottom can, they could blast a tennis ball almost into outer space with all the "boom" of a real cannon!

A few days before we left, we mothers had all sewed red stripes down blue-jean pant legs and put gold buttons on dark blue shirts to add a touch of authenticity, and had made droopy little cocked hats that satisfied their imaginations. There were other little boys who had come from near and far, and were willing to be wound up in old sheets to add a touch to the battlefield. A tent with a red cross had been erected. They'd made stretchers out of dining-table leaves. I could hardly believe what I saw! It was like watching a setting of "our gang" in real life.

And about that time, Larry came swinging into the kitchen looking for all the world like Abe Lincoln with his black hair, bushy beard, serious eyes, high cheek bones, and angular frame! I didn't know whether to run out into the yard and save the flag that was going down in defeat, or to hand Larry an envelope so he could put some finishing touches on the Gettysburg Address!

Many times people have asked why the boys are so interested in the Civil War, and I really don't have an answer. I only know that somehow it has fired their imagination. And many people have noticed the likness of Larry to Lincoln, specially when he was in a play and walked onto the stage in a black coat and top hat. (The beard then was not real. The one today is.) The audience gasped, for the likeness to Lincoln was so amazing. A year or so ago we found out why. A relative of ours had copies made of our family tree and discovered that Abraham Lincoln's Aunt Margaret (sister to his mother, Nancy Hanks) was one of our great-grandmothers on mom's side of the house! That isn't of earthshaking significance, but when you stop to consider that one of our ancestors was the grandfather of Lincoln, you can begin to see there is a remote reason why there could be a likeness.

And, in the natural, all this could be very pleasing. But lineage means nothing to the Lord. The only important thing in His sight is being adopted into the family of God. Because of this, Gene told me to put the framed family tree papers in a drawer, so as not to gender pride in ancestry. "And besides," he added slyly, "I need time to find out for sure that *my* grandmother's name wasn't Wilkes or Booth!"

21

Another unhappy young wife just left. The stories are all pretty much the same—misunderstanding, refusal of either spouse to die to self, each expecting more from the other than the other can give. And I'm sure I told her many of the things I have recorded for you in this book. And somehow, I feel that God used what I had to say.

As I sat here rocking (doesn't that categorize me in a hurry?), my mind went back many years. I remember how I pulled the same boner Moses pulled. You recall, he knew in his heart God was going to use him as a savior for his people (now don't misunderstand, I'm not tagging myself with any such title. Just hang in there); so when he came on an Egyptian fighting with a Hebrew, he stepped in and slew the Egyptian. Later, he saw two Hebrews fighting, and decided to step in and start "saving his people" right off the bat! Was he ever in for a surprise! The Hebrews turned on him and accused him of desiring to slay them as he had slain the Egyptian. And here he thought it had all been done in secrecy! He fled for his life and sulked (for about forty years, I think).

The connection between myself and Brother Moses? Well, I guess I've always had this same desire to help people, especially in the area of marriage relationships. And many years ago, I heard of a young couple having problems. In fact, someone said to me, "Char, I think you should talk to her. She really needs some advice." (That was back before I realized that unasked-for advice becomes criticism in the eyes of the other person.)

And so, one day, thinking that I wanted to do my bit and initiate the "calling" I thought God had placed on my life, I contacted this dear young wife and proceeded to tell her that "I was available to talk with her whenever she wished, and could we get together sometime?" (Oh, how gracefully my halo enshrined my little puffed-up head!)

There was a pause at the other end of the phone. I was quite sure she was wiping away tears of gratitude when out of her mouth streamed cursings, fury, threats—I could hardly believe my sanctified ears. And did I ever learn a vital lesson! It is one thing to know in your heart what God has called you to do, but the test of maturity is to wait until He says *the time is right!* I learned the hard way that God prepares the person, then sends her to you! He really doesn't need our manipulating, only our willingness, but that isn't the same as *pushiness*! How I praise the Lord for lessons learned, even if they were learned the hard way. I can truly look back and say, "Thanks, Lord—I needed that!"

22

Oh, how I hug the simplicity of Christ to me! Gone are the days of complexity, the days of making simple things hard. And here to stay are the thoughts that gender rest, peace, joy, and all the other fruits of the Spirit.

Now, don't you think that is a "good confession"? Of course it is. And it can be the confession of your mouth also, if you will just come to see that your problems start in your thought life. Get your thinking straight, and your life will become one of blessing to yourself, and to others as well.

I like to put it this way. "If you *think* right, you will *do* right. If you *do* right, you will *feel* right." And then you will have yourself under control (temperance, one of the fruits of the Spirit).

I think it all began in my life when I was reading a book by Madame Guyon. I can't recall the incident word for word, but I remember that she was riding in a carriage, and a young man by the name of Fenelon got into the carriage with her. As I recall, he was somehow repulsed by this rather aggressive woman, but he was so taken with her words and her quiet understanding of the things of God that he had to finally admit that she had a close walk with God. As I remember, she came to be a tremendous blessing to him and was the instrument of God that would be used to raise him to great heights of spiritual blessing.

Women, take hope! God has raised up a woman or two to get His work done in the past. Did you know Watchman Nee came to Christ through a woman preacher and that his mother was a powerful evangelist? His greatest source of inspiration down through the years came through a Miss Margaret Barber. And, after a charismatic experience, when the Chinese brothers started thinking that women should be "quiet in the church," the "brothers" would put up a sheet between the women and themselves, and then would sit close to the sheet in order to hear the words of blessing that came from the sisters as they taught the other sisters. It seems they wanted to be on safe Scriptural grounds of not being taught by a woman.

But back to Fenelon and Madame Guyon.

The sentence that caught my heart was simply when she stated the fact that "the kingdom of God is within you." It really started the thoughts churning within Fenelon and within myself as well. I don't think I fully understood the portent of these words at that time, but now realize that they had to lie on my heart like "the rain cometh down, and the snow from heaven, and . . . watereth the earth" (Isa. 55:10). I had to let these words rest on my heart like snow until the warmth of God's love and His growth within me caused these words to "melt" into my heart and become a part of my life.

Of course most of you will recognize these few words about the kingdom of God as being found in Luke 17:21, but let me share it with you from the Amplified. "For behold, the kingdom of God is within you (in your hearts) and among you (surrounding you)."

And then one day it began to dawn on me! The "kingdom of God" was "within me," and the keys to this kingdom were my attitudes! Truly, I held the keys to my own happiness right within my own breast; and I could, with God's tender, loving guidance, step into this kingdom which was indeed a land flowing with milk and honey, with luscious fruit set before me (the fruits of the Spirit—love, joy, peace, longsuffering, gentleness, goodness, meekness, faith, and temperance, or self-control).

Now, I had to face squarely the fact that the land which was flowing with milk and honey still had formidable giants that were stalking my very spiritual life. But I began to grasp from the Word of God that I needn't be concerned with the giants in the land, because the battle was the Lord's and He would fight the battles for me, if I would only enter into His rest!

I feel that I entered into His rest when I firmly, solidly, trustingly put my feet into the Jordan and saw the waters parting as I received the baptism in the Holy Spirit. Now, you can scream, squirm, and fight against that experience all you want to, but no matter how loudly you protest, I will go down to my last breath thanking and praising God for this experience, for it was like stepping through a door into another land that was bright with promise. When I stepped through this door, the first thing I saw was the need for developing mature attitudes, which is a means of getting a firm hold onto "holiness," without which *no one shall see the Lord!*

I'm sure it goes without saying that any kingdom of God must have Christ reigning on the throne. Now, if you are situated squarely on the throne within your heart, then it cannot be the kingdom of *God*. It is then the kingdom of *self*.

But assuming that Christ is reigning there, then each thought should be brought captive to Him, to see if these thoughts are going to render the proper attitudes that would naturally go along with Christ-likeness.

And so, I learned to examine my thoughts. Does this thought bring peace to my heart? Or does it gender bitterness? Should I keep it or toss it out? Are my thoughts about a certain person thoughts of goodness or thoughts of resentment? Can I see this person as someone who has been created in the image of God and as a fallen creature like myself? Or do I see him as not as good as myself? (Any self-righteous thoughts cannot be tolerated! They must be banished from the kingdom!)

Then I discovered that the policy of the kingdom is to "love the Lord your God with all your heart" (keeping your heart with all diligence, for out of it are the issues of life) "and with all your soul, and with all your strength and with all your mind" (Luke 10:27 Amp.). This was engraved on the ceiling of the castle within my heart. On the side walls of the castle in broad strokes were the words that proclaimed, "and thou shalt love thy neighbor as thyself."

I knew I needed a lot of work on this, because I didn't have a self-image that was all that good, and I knew I'd never be able to love others until I began to see myself as something unique and precious in the eyes of God, so that I could agree with Him and begin to see others in the same light!

I believe that my starting place was simply in trusting God to have the ability to do what He said He would do. He said He would transform me, if I would co-operate by renewing my mind. Renewing to me meant redoing. I would have to redo my thought life. I knew now that I must begin to think differently if I was going to work hand in hand with God in a willing, functioning relationship.

My outlook from the kingdom windows had previously been bad. In my immaturity, I had always looked on my circumstances negatively: too much work, and not fulfilling enough, so many children, and not enough of my husband; always tired and irritable; so little joy but with an outside cloak of humor to wear as my cover-up—that didn't. So often piqued by having to do for others, and quite often thinking they were taking advantage of me or my hospitality. (Oh, how I robbed myself of so many blessings!)

But when I began to look at these circumstances as coming directly from God's hand as a means of making me grow up in Him, how my life changed!

I began to see each child no longer as a burden but as a blessing. I saw my husband as representing Christ in my home, and that any good thing I could do for him was the same as doing it for Christ, and for His very own sake! I saw my husband as created in the image of God, though a fallen creature just like myself. We complemented one another in a beautiful way as my weaknesses were my husband's strengths, and his weaknesses were somehow my strengths, and that together we became a "whole."

I began to see my work as a blessed challenge, thanking and praising God for even the most mundane tasks around the house because anything that was done heartily and as unto the Lord carried such a blessing with it that my heart could learn to sing and be blessed even while cleaning out the johnny! Indeed, I could be just as happy as queen of the latrine as I could be being queen of this domain!

One of Gene's favorite sayings is "Ladies, you treat your husband like a king, and he will happily treat you like a queen." And then I laughingly look at him and ask, "Why does this queen feel so often like a lady-in waiting when you have to be gone on the road so much?'' But the laughter is good natured because even this difficult assignment—of being his lady-in-waiting—is something I've been able to hand to the Lord, for I've finally come to realize that each man must have the right to decide how he will provide for his family. If it means family separations for short periods of time, we can thank and praise God each time He brings our husband back to us. We can thank God that the separation has not been for all of time and that He is still the blessed controller of all things, caring more for us than we could ever care for ourselves. We can then see these circumstances as being a means of blessing instead of balking against the will of God.

But it all goes back again to heart attitudes. Get your attitudes straight before the Lord, and then out of these proper attitudes will flow the ''issues of life.'' If you see each task as a blessing instead of a chore; if you see each child as something to be shaped and conformed into the image of Christ; if you see your neighbors as fallen creatures like yourself (instead of thinking of yourself as better than they are because you know Christ); if you see each day as being handed to you from God to be a blessing to others and if you see yourself as standing in the gap between God and your unsaved loved ones, not as a preacher of righteousness but as an intercessor, believing in your heart that the ''effectual fervent prayer of a righteous man availeth much''; if you catch the vision that *righteousness* means the ''right way of doing and thinking'' and that unrighteousness is the ''wrong way of doing and thinking''; then you will come to realize that ''as a man thinketh in his heart, so is he!''

And all the people said *Amen*!

Bringing a book into the world is much like having a baby. Only labor pains, instead of being three minutes apart, are more like three months apart as your creation makes its rounds from publisher to publisher, before it finally settles into the lap of one of them. (There is one important difference, though: with a baby you can induce labor!) Contractions are felt in your throat, and breathing becomes more difficult every time you see the mailman approaching.

I suppose you could say the period of gestation begins when you find yourself staring into space more than usual from your favorite rocker, and discover the children are having to call your name three times before you answer with "oh, huh?" And when you are *really* beginning to pick up steam and formulate some ideas, you'll hear from a far distance such things as "Mom, it's your turn to drive the team to the game. Mom, Jamie-is-playing-with-matches-in-the-front-room-and-see-you're-not-even-listening-you-never-do-when-you're-writing-a-book."

You then move from the embryonic thinking stage to the fetal-producing stage. That would be the growing pile of tear-stained papers at your left elbow complete with coffee rings that resemble facial outlines, and miles of blue penciling that look like veins. At close range it is completely unintelligible, looking as though it should be decoded, which my reliable little niece in Newburgh does, when she isn't beating her head against the wall. (I've told her she shouldn't cry so much while using an electric typewriter unless she wears rubber gloves, and she said she wouldn't if I'd quit sending everything in cryptogram. She complained once, "Why do your first drafts always look like you'd just washed your hands and couldn't do a thing with them? I've the only fingers in town with fallen arches!")

And we both agree that our lives would have been simpler if I'd never gotten the urge to write. Yet, we also both agree that there is nothing more disturbing than unfulfilled creativity. I felt I had a clear word from the Lord and that the desire to write came from His heart first and then settled into mine; so I had to be on with His work that was set before me.

I remember well the many frustrations I went through before *If You See Lennie* came into being. At times, I'd wonder why I'd ever thought I could write. There were desperate moments when I thoughtfully considered hanging myself from the front hall tree, but knew instinctively that I'd never be missed—*or* noticed, what with fifty-six doorknobs available and always beckoning to soaring caps, scarves, and what-not. So I gave that up and just cried buckets of tears instead.

But then, one golden shimmering day, my one literary achievement that didn't abort made its way into the publisher's and came out again as a real, actual entity, complete with cover, title, and price tag.

It all happened on a vibrant April day about 11:30 A.M. Mark had lost his lunch money and so had pedaled up to the front step at the same moment the mailman was trying to wad a lumpy package into the mailbox. Mark took a quick peek at the return address, dialed me at Judy's (we were wallpapering her bathroom), and exclaimed, "Mom! It's here—I know this is it! Can I open it?"

"No! Don't cut the cord—I mean, wait until I get there! I'll be right home!" It took both Judy and me to extricate the phone out of my hand as I am the world's messiest paperhanger. I remember hollering, "Judy, I'll see you later! I have to go have a book—I mean a look," as I shuffled out of her house bearing a strong resemblance to a Yukon explorer due to gobs of wallpaper stuck to both feet which caused me to break and accelerate at the same time. Fortunately, I didn't live too far away, or my guardian angel would have rebelled, I'm sure. I parked in the garage, picked the paper off my shoes and tried to brush the dried paste from the front of my jeans. After all, I was now a published author, and inside that house my adoring public was waiting for me. (Mark had called in the married part of the clan for the grand opening.) I needed to appear calm and unruffled, as though this was an everyday occurrence—which was outright hypocrisy because I wanted to get on the rooftop and shout it to the whole neighborhood!

But in a way, I was bracing myself for their reaction. I remembered the day sixteen months before when I'd stood before them, patted my halo, hung my head with just the right touch of humility and made the quiet statement that "something rather unusual happened to me today on my way out to the mailbox. I mailed a signed contract to do a book."

"Neat, mom. What's for supper?"

Groan.

"Be sure to leave me out of your story. No offense, mom."

And from my thoughtful husband: "Hmmm. Wonder if I'll become known as Mr. Charlene Potterbaum?"

"Yeah, great, mom. Did you remember to sew up my pants?" et cetera.

But on this "day of delivery" I saw new respect in their eyes. In just twenty-four hours I went from "Hey, you" to "Mother, dear." Basking in my new role as published author I primly mentioned that "after all, it is perfectly Scriptural—the Bible states that 'her children will rise up and call her blessed.' " To which one thoughtful offspring mumbled, "I dunno, mom. It sure would be hard to call you 'blessed' after calling you 'mom' all these years" And with that I went to sew up more torn pants, but with a warmer glow than before (in fact, I was sure I must be shimmering) because now I knew that the dream had become a reality. Not a dream, really, but a vision. God had shown me so many, many years before this that someday I would write a book. It was a longing, a desire, that I knew He would honor.

And as I sat there, sewing up torn pants as "unto the Lord," I realized something—that may help many of you who are reading this book. I realized that much of the inner turmoil I had felt at times was an unnameable, unwordable frustration because I knew that deep inside I was cradling an ability that needed to be used for

God. It had taken much travailing prayer to bring this "thing" forth because it was buried so deep, under mountains of self-love and wedged in the crevices of "Who me, Lord? Impossible!"

My heart's cry to you is don't shrink from the shaping (otherwise known as chastening) of the Lord. Don't shrink for one moment from those hands of love that long to make and mold you into something usable. You may not be able to tell others about the things He has whispered to you. There may not be another living soul with whom you can share the "great things" God lets you know are stored up for you, but never lose sight of them. They are stored up for you in Jesus and they are lying on your heart for *His* glory!

Yes, bringing a book into the world *is* much like having a baby, for it came complete with its own particular problems. It meant being awakened in the middle of the night by distraught housewives who were certain that, because I'd written a book, I'd have all the answers. It meant giving the milk of the Word to some because they couldn't stand "strong meat," and it meant burping any number because of spiritual indigestion. It also meant spending hours in a cramped position as you straddled atop some ill-fitting pedestal someone had perched you on. But I soon discovered that pedestal-perching could quickly give one varicose veins, so I quit that in a hurry. And yes, I even had to be weaned away from the book. I had to see it as God's tool to use as He saw fit, and not as something I could boast about.

And people do the strangest things. After a speaking engagement someone will rush up to me and I'll think, "How sweet. She is going to greet me with a holy kiss," only to have her move in close and count "one, two, three! She *does* have only three eyelashes."

Many people ask "Is Lennie for real?" (She is.) And "How do you think she will feel when she finds you've written a book of letters to her?" And I tell them, "Her first reaction would be, 'You know, that's just like Char. Anything to save the postage!' "

Well, personally, I think everyone should write a book. Oh, granted, you get into tight spots sometimes. You can begin to feel very egotistical about the whole thing. *My* book, *my* testimony, *my* children, *my* experiences, and so on. But isn't this what it's all about—being a witness to what He has done for you, declaring to all who will listen that "I have not hid thy righteousness within my heart; I have declared thy faithfulness and thy salvation: I have not concealed thy lovingkindness and thy truth from the great congregation" (Ps. 40:10)?

No, I'd rather know that I had endeavored to say it all, no matter how poorly, than to have it stuffed in my heart to shrivel up inside me. It is with overwhelming gratitude that I can point to that first book and say, "Thanks, Lord—I needed that!" For it speaks to me of His faithfulness, of His desire to work cooperatively with me, His child, and of His willingness to use me, in spite of my glaring imperfections. You see, He is a good God. A very, very good God.

24

Laurie made a brief appearance at my prayer group's meeting last night to drop off some books. I tried not to burst with pride when she came through the door so vivacious and full of bubbly enthusiasm. She sparkled at us, spoke a few words, dropped the books into my lap, and breezed out of the door. We all sensed that a breath of fresh air had blown our way.

I couldn't help thinking about her as I drove home. And suddenly I realized something. The scar! The ugly scar had been completely covered over and was no longer noticeable! And with a sweet sense of gratitude, my memories raced back in time to the awful moment when I thought we'd lost her forever.

When I got home, I shuffled through a stack of yellowed papers until I found . . . yes, here it is, the story of our near heartbreak of the summer of 1968. Let me share it with you.

As we live on a main artery, sirens are not an uncommon sound to us. They often cut through the air in pursuit of some speeder or en route to a pesky grass fire. But a quick glance at the pinched face of my thirteen-year-old Janis as she came running to me told me the siren I had taken for granted only moments before held a particular heartache for me.

"Mother, it's Laurie! She's been hit by a car!"

A strange, faraway feeling came over me. My eight-year-old . . . struck by a car . . . busy highway. I had frequently wondered what this dreaded moment would feel like.

101

From what seemed like a great distance, I heard voices talking. They were telling me that my husband was already at the scene of the accident and that *I was not to go to her*. Somehow, the terrible impact of the words seemed to buffet me back to consciousness, and the faraway feeling left me. I knew that I had to go to her immediately, no matter what anyone said. In fact I remember feeling a torrent of rage toward them and I was shaking violently.

A neighbor offered to drive me down to the small grocery where the accident had happened, but before we could even get out of the driveway the ambulance sped by with my little girl and her daddy inside.

As we raced to the hospital close behind the ambulance, I tried to keep my mind busy. I kept the most fearful thoughts out by trying to see God's hand in all this. But uppermost in my mind was the question, *"Why Laurie, Lord?"*

Laurie was our "in-betweener," the fourth child of our six. She was just coming out of that dimply baby stage that grandparents find so adorable. Now well into the exasperating stage where whining and peevishness thrive, the remaining bit of little girl in her was still longing for the attention she had at one time enjoyed.

Our teen-agers were all absorbed in their individual worlds. They stepped into ours only occasionally to cuddle the two youngest who were still loaded with baby charm—but more often, to snap at Laurie and send her away in tears. I'll admit, she cried too loudly and too often. It was her plea for more understanding, but we didn't respond to her plea.

I saw it had been urgently necessary for God to speak sharply through the dreaded siren to reach our hearts. It was the only way He could get our attention and make us face squarely the unfairness of partiality.

As we made our way to the hospital, I prayed, "Oh please, Lord, give me another chance. I've been so blind."

Another thought caused me a great deal of uneasiness. We had been neglecting family devotions. I had left most of her religious training to her Sunday school teachers. Other thoughts crowded in. I thought of all the vitamins and physical check-ups I had considered so important for her. Of what value were they to either of us when at this very moment she might be in eternity?

Through my tears, the outline of the hospital finally came into view. The nurse on duty took us immediately to the emergency room. Before I got to the door, I could hear her crying softly. It was not the cry of a whiny, peevish, frightened little child. It was the cry of a bewildered girl who didn't even know what had hit her.

Once I realized she was still alive, I knew I had to pull a smile out of the depths of my being somehow. I couldn't do much about my red, swollen eyes, but I knew I had to act calm and natural.

My first impulse was to hug her to me tightly, but a quick look told me there wasn't one huggable spot unbandaged.

As they took the bandages off, I had to leave the room. I was afraid I was going to be sick. The headlight ornament of the '59 Chevy that had struck her had torn an ugly gash across her forehead, just above the left eye. It looked as though the eyebrow was gone completely, and the bone of the forehead crushed. I thought "Oh, God! It could have been her *eye.*"

I knew her beauty had been marred for life, and no doubt her face would be badly disfigured. I shook myself. "God has spared her life and you are concerned about her vanity?"

The surgeon came. The minutes melted into hours as we waited and paced. After they had sutured the puncture, examined and X-rayed her aching body, we were able to take her home. There were no broken bones nor any internal injuries. An obvious miracle, as we had just gotten word from the officers that she had been thrown thirty feet. Statistically, she should have died from the impact!

Oh, the newspapers made it sound so simple. "Treated and released." There was no mention of the sad little girl who neither talked nor smiled for three days. Nor could they know of the deep lessons learned by well-meaning, procrastinating parents.

Yes, the doctor had mended her body. But God had again put the welfare of her soul back into our keeping. Every glance at the ugly scar takes the edge out of my tone, puts new love in my touch.

I'm striving to be more patient. I'm learning to live in closer touch with Him. Should He ever speak to me through a siren again, I don't want to live forever with the memory that I didn't do for them spiritually what God would have every Christian parent do.

Believe me, the lesson has been engraved on my heart for life. But praise God, the scar is gone!

103

25

Did you know that it is one of the mercies of the Lord that we can't smell our own garlic-tainted breath? Just brought that up because I'm munching on a garlicky bit of snack mix that would be most offensive to my husband—if he were here. He has gone to Chicago on business and though I comfort myself with the fact that he will be back in two days, I am experiencing the verse in Genesis that says "your desire *and craving* shall be for your husband, and he shall rule over you" (Amplified: italics mine).

Oh, how I praise the Lord for this desiring and craving that has been given me for the one human being that is the other part of me! And how I prasie the Lord that this very "desiring and craving" that was actually a part of the curse becomes such blessing when tempered by the Holy Spirit and under His control. My husband's "having the rule" over me is the very protection, the very covering I need for my ultimate safety.

What a plan! What wisdom, what grace this God provides. Is it any wonder my heart sings continually? Oh, world! Have you seen the change in this poor creature? Do you remember the insecure, anxiety-ridden neurotic of the past? Oh, truly the Lord is restoring the years that the "locust hath eaten." It's no wonder that the Lord has given me whole troops of faithful readers, because all of this joy could not be contained in one vessel. It "must needs" be shared!

And I suppose the one thought that makes me more deliriously happy than any other is the precious secret I discovered (a spiritual law I see emerging) that as I am becoming the kind of woman I have always wanted to be (due to the working of the Spirit of God within me), I see my husband becoming the kind of husband I have always wanted *him* to be.

You see, the problem never really was with him, although I tried to convince the Lord in the secret places of my heart that our marriage problems were there because Gene was "not as spiritual" as I thought he should be. (Ugly words, those. I almost dread seeing them in print.)

I even remember having the audacity to tell him that I didn't think he read his Bible enough. To which my Lord and Savior thundered back at me, "Now listen to me, wife of his youth. It is not how much of the Bible you *read* that is important to me, it is *how much of it you obey that matters to Me!*

Meekly, I saluted my Master and dropped that self-righteous attitude as one would drop a rank garment. I went to my dear husband and asked his forgiveness, fully acknowledging that even though I read the Word more than he did he never held resentments as I do, didn't say hurtful words about others as quickly as I, and always he was quicker to defend others when they were being criticized. And then, though it smarted a bit, I had to admit to him (and to myself) that my own particular proneness to sinning was of such a nature that it took floods and floods of His word to keep me continually cleansed and functioning properly.

Well, as you can see, I learn many of my lessons the hard way. And so, each morning I curl up beside him and whisper, "Honey, today I want to be a good wife. A really good wife. I know I will never be a spotless housekeeper or a perfect mother, but oh, I'm convinced I have the makings of a good wife and God has given me today to prove myself!" Gene always holds me a bit closer to show his approval, and we just talk about the day, its problems, some solutions, what he hopes to get done.

And guess what? Neither of us looks too great. Our hair is always rumpled, and I dearly love the feeling of his overnight growth of beard against my cheek. And I love the feeling of security and acceptance all this gives to me. And I would like to think that it gives him a feeling of being needed and respected. And always, it gives us both a feeling of His presence, for God is love.

Is it any wonder that my desiring and craving is "unto him," this special gift from God, my husband?

26

I'd gone to shop at a new mall in a nearby town. I thought it would be a great chance to have lunch with an old school chum who lived in the same town. She met me at the mall, and my, how good it was to talk.

We did a bit of small talking at first, then she sheepishly told me her little secret—a secret which nearly toppled me off my chair.

She said, "Char, I don't think you realized what I just said. Max and I are about to have our seventh child!"

"Babs, I heard you. It just took a while to register!" Babs had lockered near me in school—that would make her forty-two, as she'd been a year behind me. I congratulated her and told her how great it was.

We went on with our conversation, then something caught my ear. I heard her say, "Since I'll be having the baby by Caesarian section, I . . ."

I was baffled, and I'm sure it showed. "Babs, you never told me you had any children by Caesarian. Why did this happen?" (Why do I always have to be so morbidly curious and blurt everything out that way?)

Slowly, and with great deliberation, Babs put her fork down. She looked me straight in the eye, and with a measured tone she confided, "Because, Char, I committed abortion two years ago."

I tried valiantly not to look shocked. A long, silent moment passed, and I said astutely, "oh-h." Then I reached across the table and touched her hand. "Babs, you didn't have to answer such a stupid question. Please forgive me. All that has happened in your past is under the blood of Christ, and I had no right to pry such a confession out of you.''

We quietly resumed our eating. ''Char, I needed to be able to look you right in the eye and tell you that. Just for that very reason—because it *is* all under the blood. Do you know what it does to me, knowing the depth of His sweet forgiveness? I, of all people, can comprehend beyond the shadow of a doubt that my heart is desperately wicked. But how grateful I am for a God who was willing to send His Son to die in my place. I know now I can stand free and clear from the guilt that used to cause me such agony before I came to Christ. Well, at any rate, I wracked myself up but good! So, they will have to take the child by Caesarian.''

We both felt we should get to a more cheerful topic, so we quickly changed the conversation. But when I walked out of the restaurant, I couldn't help thinking of the many, many women who have done such a thing and don't know of the cleansing, precious forgiveness that Christ offers to sinners. I wondered how many women wake up at night with nightmares they can't face. I wondered how many emotional ills are due to tightly locked up secrets that can't be told out of fear of shocking others, or destroying ''self-images.'' Teen-agers, in particular, face these problems. They are turned loose in a world of immorality, ''free love'' flaunted from the screen, an ''everybody's doing it'' approach, experimentation, and the result for many is conception.

Some have come to me with venereal disease. Some have come because they are pregnant. And some have come simply because the pressure of guilt from premarital sex has been more than they could handle.

For the most part, I become a listener. But also, I become a counselor in the truest sense of the word. For, to counsel, according to Webster, is the ''act of exchanging ideas.''

Dear ones, I'm not their judge. I can only be a means of helping them to see the long-term outcome of their decisions. But ultimately, the decision must be theirs and theirs alone. Parents, also, are often the deciding factor.

And, because we are human, we often lose sight of the real crime. The *real* crime, the basic sin, is *Christ-rejection*, not abortion or premarital sex. Really, can we expect anything more than sinful actions from the unregenerate heart?

I've seen venereal disease bring a young girl to Christ. I've had others decide on abortion. I've had some abstain from premarital sex after experiencing forgiveness. And, I've also had some go on with the loose morals, carefree and laughing. For how long, I ask myself. But I've loved them all! And so has God.

27

We were at the obstetrician's office. Jan and I had been smiling over some cartoons we'd come across in a magazine. It felt good to smile, my heart was so heavy with concern for Jan. Complications had arisen. She looked so fresh and crisp in her maternity clothes—wished I didn't have this feeling in the pit of my stomach. She's waited four years for a baby. Motherly concern doesn't lessen when they get married. *Lord, why do I ache inside?*

Jan had struck up a conversation with the matching mother-and-daughter pair across from us. I couldn't help wonder, *is that mother's heart aching, too?*

Then I heard Jan mentioning the cost of delivery, around three hundred dollars, I think she said. I knew I needed to concentrate on conversation.

The other mother said, "My, it hardly seems possible! My last baby was born about four years ago. It only cost me about one hundred and seventy-five—high cost of living, I guess."

"No," Jan smiled. "I think you could say it is the high cost of loving!"

And we were ushered into the doctor's office. Only moments later we heard the doctor saying what our hearts were fearing: She was in danger of going into delivery at any moment and more than likely it would be a *placenta previa* birth. Now each day must be handed to God, and we must grasp securely the fact that truly, He *is* the blessed controller of all things; not only our times are in His hands but our hopes, our dreams, and now, even this unborn child.

(one week later)

Though it saddens our hearts,
there will be no grandbaby in May.
As Dr. Ketcham stated: "God is too kind and
loving to be cruel, and He is likewise too wise
to make a mistake."
May Jesus Christ be praised!
Our Jan is fine, and looking
to the future.
Amen

28

God may have granted Gene and me some ability to handle problems *after* the marriage, but He seems to have given my brother, Allen, a pretty great talent also. Matchmaking!

We were over there for coffee yesterday and he was grinning broadly about the most recent bit of matchmaking he'd done. He reported that all was going well; the couple seemed to be starry-eyed with just the hint of wedding bells in the near future. And then we all giggled as we recounted how Gene and I had helped dear brother Allen on one of these ventures several years ago.

It went something like this: Allen had stopped in for coffee and was wearing a proud grin as he told me that one of the young couples whom he'd introduced to one another had just been blessed with their first baby after a few years of marriage, and that they named the baby after his daughter, Kay Lynn. We were showering Allen with words of encouragement and admiration, telling him how excited he must feel to be the instrument God used to bring these two together.

Allen admitted, "Yep! I'm real pleased the way their marriage has turned out, if I do say so myself! Now, I've got another real fine girl who works in our office. She's about twenty-eight or thirty and I can just tell she'd really like to be married someday. I'd sure like to find some nice guy for her."

Gene looked thoughtful. "Did you say about thirty? Hmmm."

I raised one eyebrow and said, "Now what? Our kids aren't that old and we've run out of single cousins. What do you have in mind, kind sir?''

''I was just thinking about Joe, my barber; I overheard him say something the other day. He was listening as I told him some of the crazy things the kids have done and he very wistfully said, 'I'm ready to settle down. You make me long for a home and a wife more than ever.'

Well, it didn't take me more than thirty seconds to get on the bandwagon! We began to question Allen. It seemed as though the height was about right, and the age was perfect—she was about thirty and Joe, the barber, was thirty-five. Neither had ever been married, and both had expressed a desire to find ''someone.'' Both were extremely good looking and neat in appearance, with just enough spunk to consider a blind date made by someone they could trust.

We had a great time as we sat there thinking of the possibilities. The very next day, Allen asked her if she would consider a date if he made the arrangements; and she said, ''Hey, you're quite famous around here for good matches—sure, I'll go! What's his name?''

My brother looked a bit sheepish as he admitted, ''I know this sounds wild, but we got so enthusiastic about this being a great match, I completely forgot to get his last name! But I know Gene said his name was Joe.''

She laughed. ''That's a great start already, because one of my favorite people is named Joe.'' Allen assured her he'd find out more details, now that he knew she'd not be offended if we made a meeting possible.

In the meantime, Gene went over to Joe's barber shop. Joe should have been suspicious, as Gene didn't really need a haircut.

So Gene settled back in the chair and began a very leisurely conversation with poor, unsuspecting Joe.

''Joe, I couldn't help think about you the other day. You mentioned wanting to find someone. Would you be offended if we sort of—well, made an arrangement, so to speak.'' And so he blithely stammered his way through the conversation—this smooth, closes-every-sale salesman of mine! (Gene later remarked, ''Well, I felt a bit out of my element, and after all, he *did* have scissors in his hand!'')

It took us a few days to get back together with Allen again. He came by, and we all began to share how we'd felt them both out, and they seemed to be at least willing to consider a blind date.

And I kept sputtering things like, "Now, Allen, you realize that we never do things like this. I'm only going on your complete success with this kind of thing; I don't really approve of this way of meeting—but it *is* kind of exciting, isn't it!''

We proceeded to put our bits of information together, and were about to make some arrangements when Allen said, "Char, I never did catch his last name. Who is he?''

Enthusiastically, Gene said, "Oh, you know Joe. Joe Bizzano. I've—'' but his voice trailed off as Allen absolutely doubled up with laughter and roared with hilarity to such an extent that he almost fell out of his chair. We racked our brains trying to think of what could be so uproarious about a simple name like Joe Bizzano!

And then, finally, when he could get control of himself he wiped the tears from his eyes and said brokenly and between great guffaws, "Did you say Bizzano?''

And when we nodded affirmatively, he doubled up again but tried to tell us as best he could without choking to death that "*her* name is—is—*Mary Bizzano*!'' (you guessed it—brother and sister!)

Then we were all beyond anyone's control as we began to add up what could have happened if we'd proceeded with plans and had gotten these two together because they both still lived at home with their parents, and we could just see the two of them getting ready for a blind date on the same night. Well, you have your own imagination and your own tear ducts, so you improvise your own ideas. But isn't living fun?

29

My lithe, bronzed sixteen-year-old Laurie just slithered by me. I sighed. Was I ever that young? That slim? I know I was never that tan, as tanning just isn't for me. The only part of my anatomy that is ever permanently tanned is my right hand, from reaching into the mailbox every hour on the hour until the mail has arrived.

The only other way I'd ever get a tan would be to put a sun lamp in the refrigerator! Summers around here seem to be one long smorgasbord. And now that summer has happened, I'm trying desperately to adjust to it. In one fell swoop I went from quiet, tranquil days to bedlam. At this moment there is a drum thumping upstairs, cornet blaring downstairs, doorbells are a-ringing, phones ding-a-linging, can openers whirring, cake mixes stirring, and a kitten yowling in-a-pear-tree. . . .

The path from here to the summer porch looks like a Hansel and Gretel trail strewn with potato chip bags, candy wrappers, hair rollers, and apple cores. I wish I could tell you that my children are well-trained and always remember to pick up these things, but I'd probably be struck by a thunderbolt from heaven if I did. You see, I'd rather praise God because they *sometimes* remember to pick these things up, rather than go all to pieces because they don't *always* remember. I think that's called "being positive." I call it remaining sane, in spite of everything.

The Bible says we should "be instant in season, out of season; reprove, rebuke, exhort with all longsuffering and doctrine" (2 Tim. 4:2 KJV); and a few verses later we read, "I have fought a

114

good fight, I have finished my course, I have kept the faith." It's a good thing they've never asked me to paraphrase this passage. I'd come up with something like this: "Keep your cool when they are in school, and when they are out. Reprove. Rebuke. Exhort, all you like. But in the end you will suffer long. I have fought a good fight—they almost threw me off course, but at least I've kept the faith."

And then I hear a gentle voice saying, "Lo, children are a heritage from the Lord, the fruit of the womb a reward." And I whisper, "Thanks, Lord—I needed that!"

30

About here, the superspiritual and the intellectual saint may want to leave us, temporarily at least. This is only for those who refused to throw wit and humor out when they gave up coarse jokes and foolish jesting. This is a fragment from real life—*my* real life.

It happened several years ago, when we lived across the street from our store. It was a ghastly hot and humid summer day when God began testing us to see if we were rejoicing in Him, or in the fact that we were comfortably cool at all times; for the air-conditioning systems went out at both the store and at home, due to burned-out fuses.

Even the store's supply of fuses had been depleted, so Gene came over to the house, handed me some money, and asked me to go down to the K-Mart just a few blocks away to pick up some fuses.

It was a reasonable request, and I loved doing something for Gene in an effort to make up for the lack I'd always felt about not having a business head to help him more in the store. So I powdered my nose, changed clothes, and as I was about to sail out the door one of the kids called, "Wait, mom! Try this great fruit concoction I put together."

It looked cool, refreshing, and very deep purple; so I slugged it down, mumbling, "Thanks, sweetheart, that was real refreshing. But don't ruin it by telling me what all you put in it! See you in just a few minutes. I won't be gone long."

I found the needed fuses, and stood in a long line that was getting longer by the minute. Finally, it was my turn at the check-out counter. The clerk, who'd seemed a bit bored previously, looked up at me and grinned. Naturally, I thought she must be sensing the presence of God in me, so I smiled sweetly and she said—a bit giggly— "that will be $2.46."

But when I reached into my purse, I discovered that I'd left my billfold on the kitchen counter during the punch-guzzling session. I smiled even more sweetly and said, "I've left my billfold at home. It seems a bit silly, but I have my checkbook. Is it all right if I write you a check?"

"Oh, yes," still wearing that certain smile. By now, the line behind me was getting much longer. I remember wondering if all the fuses in town had blown out. I endured all the self-conscious sufferings that you go through when you are writing out a check in front of such a long line, thinking about how you hated to hold everyone up, how you were praying there'd be a balance when you went to put it in as an entry, and wishing you didn't feel so dumb when you knew others were glaring over your shoulder watching you write.

I handed her the check.

She looked at me, smiling wider than ever and said, "Thank you. Now may I see your identification?"

I think if there'd been any bit of saintly shimmering about me, it would have disappeared about then, because I said, "Honey, that's why I wrote the check. I don't *have* my billfold!" And I remember fancying her a bit dense to think that I'd have identification anywhere else *but* my billfold!

We were both still smiling, but my smile was a bit more plastic than it had been previously. I leaned toward her in a real comradely fashion, pointed to the name on the check and said earnestly, "Look, dear. Potterbaum's. We have the big store right down the street, we're neighbors. Now, if this was a forty-dollar check I was trying to pass, you might have a problem. But $2.46? Now, be a dear and find someone who can give me permission to take my fuses and go."

People behind me in line were starting to clear their throats. I glanced back, hoping they'd pity me a bit in my helplessness. My relief was great, as most of them smiled back at me, and some even snickered a little.

Well, the check-out girl directed me to someone who was evidently a bit higher up on the totem pole, in another lane. We went through the same ritual: me, a frenzied purchaser proclaiming my honesty to her, an authority figure of K-Mart! Again, I'm pointing to the check and the illustrious name of Potterbaum, emphasizing that we were practically neighbors. Finally, and with a smile, she cashed my check while again, a long line of customers had formed behind me.

I felt almost like a shoplifter as I clutched the fuses in my sweaty palm and headed toward the car. Once inside, I breathed a sigh of relief, started the car and (like I always do) adjusted the rear-view mirror. One glance into it and I gasped!

I had a ring of purple fruit punch that went almost from ear to ear! I looked like a walking "Smile-God-loves-you" button! Needless to say, this is what's known as "Mom's punch line."

I was laughing hysterically by the time I got home. Gene merely groaned and chided me, "You just *had* to give your name and tell everyone who you belonged to, didn't you!" Then he started laughing so hard, we forgot how hot it was.

Now, the deeply spiritual and the intellectual saints may go forth from here, for I have had my say about "doing my thing." It may not be all that edifying, but if it made your heart merry, my Bible says it did you good "like a medicine." So as you chuckle, I'm praying you'll exclaim, "Thanks, Lord—I needed that!"

31

One could say that the nicest thing about fastings are the days that you are not. I'll never win a Nobel prize for that last sentence but anyone who has been fasting will know what I'm trying to say.

I'm still struggling in the area of what to eat, when to say no, what is "being disciplined" and what is bordering on "being self-indulgent." I saw my doctor downtown the other day and she seemed to think I was slimming down a trifle. When she asked me if I was having any trouble, I said, "Remember how you told me I could still enjoy popcorn as long as I only had a cupful at a time? Hey, that's really generous—especially if you measure it *before* you pop it!"

And with that she went her way shaking her head and muttering to herself, no doubt scheduling me for a mental checkup!

Trudy and I were talking about this business of being disciplined as we had lunch the other day. She had come to help me for just a few hours as I needed a lift with the housework, and it turned out that she needed fellowship. She is one of the many women who have recently been deserted by their husbands.

As we ate, we talked about discipline—its value, its struggles—and without thinking, I mentioned something to her about Gene and I having a day together. I don't really remember why it got into the conversation, and so I was rather taken aback when she said quietly, "Char, for just a few quick moments there, I felt real envy creeping into my heart when you talked about you and Gene having such a good day together. What can I do about this?''

I thought a moment, then said, "Trudy, there will be many times when you will be tempted to envy others as you see them with their husbands, or hear of things they've been doing together. First of all, realize that feeling envy for just a fleeting moment could be considered just a 'temptation' as long as you don't give in to the feeling and allow it to dominate you. Second, you can make that fleeting temptation be a blessing by learning a lesson that I learned the hard way once.

"It happened a number of years ago, just after I'd received the baptism in the Holy Spirit. We'd gone to a convention in Waco, and while we were there, the Lord had given two beautiful songs to Ginger. Everyone was being so blessed by them that I felt very childish in my attitude, and a bit upset with my heavenly Father for giving my sister something He hadn't given to me.'' (This was before I'd begun to understand that He has given all of us special gifts and talents to be used as a blessing to others.)

"But since I'd come into the baptism I'd begun to grasp the idea of attitudes and their importance, and was trying to sort out the immature attitudes from substantial, mature ones. I quickly came to see that the attitude of envy I was feeling was an immature one because it had in it the attitude of 'wishing I had gotten' rather than an attitude of 'giving.' " (That is my own homemade standard of deciding which attitudes are mature and which are immature, weighing each attitude to see whether it is a "giving" attitude, as in the case of mature ones, or whether it tips the scales toward "grasping or getting" for oneself.)

"Well, I knew I needed some time with the Lord to get this thing straightened out, so I found myself a little corner where I could be alone, and I started to pray. I confessed the stirrings of envy to the Lord and asserted my willingness to give the feeling of envy up. But I thought, 'How?'

"I then realized that envying is really quite a natural inclination—a 'root' of self. Now, the only way to die to our natural inclinations is to come hard against them with an *opposite* inclination.

"And so, as I was before the Lord I prayed a prayer similar to this: 'Father, I confess the feelings of envy that are stirring around

121

on the inside and realize these feelings to be most immature. I know that You want me to become childlike, but I know there is no room in Your kingdom for childishness. So I forsake these feelings of envy right here and now by praying a most blessed and effectual ministry of music down on Ginger, a ministry that will far surpass and eclipse anything I could ever do for you. And Father, *don't let me get off my knees until I really mean it!*

"I wept as I was ashamed of my poor attitude, but it was only moments until I felt God doing a beautiful thing on the inside of me. I felt myself really and truly desiring that Ginger would have a most effective ministry and that many would be blessed by her music (which really came to pass!).

"But something else was happening. I think I was beginning to grasp a fuller meaning of 'heaping coals of fire on the head of your enemy,' for *envy* (not Ginger) was my enemy of the moment. By praying and asking God to give Ginger even more of what she already had, in spite of my feeling envious, was a way of heaping coals of fire on my enemy's head—by giving it what it didn't expect! And then it will have a sweet-smelling savor before the Lord!

"Trudy, you can do this. Every time you are tempted to envy another couple, let it be a means of heaping coals of fire on your enemy's head (envy) by asking God to bless their union in an even greater way than He already has! It will be a means of blessing for all if you follow this pattern, and it will cause the spirit of envy soon to give up if its plans backfire every time instead of causing the havoc and pain that was intended. Do you get the picture?"

Trudy did.

I also shared a profound sentence with her that I had come across as I was reading Francis Schaeffer's book *True Spirituality*. (God is always speaking to me through "profound sentences," often saying more than I can get from lengthy sermons.) This is the sentence: "We must love God enough to be content, and must love our fellow man enough not to envy." This sentence is complete in itself. What could be left of any value to add to a sentence as rich as that?

32

Believe me when I say I am not a "born" housekeeper. By nature, my inclinations are basically lazy. No, I was "born" toward beds of ease, not beds to be changed; toward procrastinating, not organizing; toward dallying, not rallying. Yet the joy of the Christian life is centered in this very challenge, to come hard against those *natural inclinations* and die to them so that the life of Christ might be more clearly evident to those about us.

I was just upstairs fluffing pillows and gathering up soiled clothing when that old urge to dislike what I was doing began to creep up on me. Sternly, I said to myself, "I'll have none of that! You'll do these things heartily, and do them as 'unto the Lord!' " And with that, I fluffed even more carefully, making mental notes of which things were first in priority, which could be put off without bordering on procrastination and could safely come under the heading of "organizing," and which things were essential and urgent.

I remembered reading somewhere that "if a woman has her dishes done and her beds made, she can't be all bad." So I knew with the final pillow fluffing I would have fulfilled that particular person's expectations.

As I was picking up and putting away anything and everything, this being Monday when things have a way of falling back into place, a few thoughts started to tumble into my mind, and I felt I wanted to share them with you.

I had just tucked a sheet under the mattress and was

straightening out on the upsweep, turning a soiled sock right side out (ugh) when the thought struck me: "Think how much you would enjoy these tasks if today were your last day to do these duties for those you love."

I'll tell you, that little gem caused a swelling in my heart that wouldn't quit. My heart became so full of gratitude and thankfulness that soon the tears were oozing down my face.

Being a "back-page scribbler" from way back, I remembered coming across a written prayer I'd seen toward the back of my Bible when I was scribbling down any number of the many things I've stashed away there.

Yes, here it is. "Lord, help us to live every day as we will wish we had when we come to die." And the tears just wouldn't stop! How could I ever complain about any of the things I have to do for this topsy-turvy, fun-loving family of mine? And another verse kept coming to mind: "So teach us to number our days that we may get us a heart of wisdom" (Ps. 90:12 Amp.).

Having no mastery of mathematics, I knew it wouldn't be possible for me to figure what number day I had reached, having eased myself into the forty-third year of my life. But I did know this much: today I was one day closer to the coming of the Lord than I was yesterday. I knew that yesterday—its failures and its flaws—was a part of my past, and that each new day is like a clean, fresh beginning. Sometimes I've mused within my heart that really we only live our lifetime in that one day. It is a biblically sound principle that each day has its own cares, its own joys, and "sufficient unto the day are the evils thereof."

And so it's a good idea to keep track of each day while it is upon us and then file it carefully away under "Day Past: recorded, and sins forgiven" (stamped and sealed by the Holy Spirit, officially). Then, you start with a nice clean slate and sail right into your errors and victories, for I am convinced that each day is full of some of each when the touch of God is on your life for all to see!

And while we are on the subject, let me share with you another printed prayer that is in the back of my Bible.

"Dear God, in the work of this day, make me decent, orderly, useful, appreciative, courageous, and kind. Let me not weaken myself by anger, cheapen myself by boasting, or play the fool by lying. Give me to remember that there are others in the world besides myself, and that they are men like unto myself. Teach me to observe the rules of the game; to come through defeat with strengthened courage and out of victory with gratitude and humility. Let me not be unmindful of the great value of friend and foe for both are much of my own making. For my own sake and for the sake of my loved ones and associates, keep me wholesome and cheerful. *But if the devil of error should grip me when mentally disturbed, grant me the good sense to go quietly alone until the impulse to act or speak unkindly shall have passed.* And at the end of each day, bring me to my bed with the knowledge that greed and malice and envy and hatred have played a lesser part in my thinking; that my weariness is the result alone of well-doing. Amen.'' (Italics are mine.)

In fact, prowling around the back of my Bible was so inspirational, I think I'd like to share some of the things I have written there with you. I can't always give proper credit to those who spoke these things, but since I know all of their hearts were right with God, they will have no objection to my sharing them with you. I'll give credit where I can.

I found this: "Incomplete obedience is disobedience."

"It's not the things that we do (sins) that makes one more worthy of hell than another—*all* are condemned."

"Christ is not valued at all until He is valued *above* all."

Hippocrates (father of medicine): "That which is used develops; that which is not, wastes away."

"Humility: when neither praise or criticism affects one."

Mumford: "*Religion* has a way of placing demands on the heart which strips it of loving mercy."

"That only is important which is eternal." (Possibly Augustine)

"Determination can eradicate distance from God." (Mull that one over awhile. It's one of those that needs to sink in a bit.)

"Submission—the absence of rebellion."

And all the people said . . . Amen!

33

Things were pretty tense last night. Markie had had the audacity to mix up some flour and water paste in the dining room, spilling some on the carpet while he was at it.

Jamie had dragged all the covers off a bed (a made bed, at that!) without permission, for a tent. And I was angry on the inside because things were not going *my* way in a marriage that I'd been counseling.

Consequently, everyone was out of sorts. Finally, my youngest son, Jamie, made this profound statement. He was walking through the kitchen and muttering, almost as if to himself. "Wow. Sure seems weird—almost as if it wasn't 'home,' or somethin'."

And like a bolt of lightening, I knew what he was thinking. Mark was nearby and had heard the comment too. I said, "Hey, fellas, that's my cue. Gather round."

They came traipsing over to me, and I put both arms around them and we just took a few minutes out with the Lord. I readily confessed to God that I had been sharp with my children and we all asked God's forgiveness for having been short with one another. Peace began to flow through our home once again. We all took some time out to work together on some Bible verses, and then into some leftover homework that hadn't been finished. Joy was restored and with it, patience and gentleness.

I know that some of you are thinking, that if your kid mixed flour and water paste in your carpeting, you'd do some haranguing, too. Well, it wasn't that I didn't reprimand, it was the unwholesome manner in which I did. My own self-love had played a most important part in the rebuke.

But after a pleasant time with the boys, I then had to quietly take stock of what had disturbed me and caused me to lose my peace. (The peace of God is to rule in our hearts; when that peace is disturbed, something else is ruling, usually "self.")

But I'd been upset by a disturbing phone call. A young couple I'd met through my first book were having troubles. The husband had been unfaithful to her and she just "couldn't get over it"; she just "knew it would never work." Now she was convinced he was "not the right one for her."

Well, naturally I didn't mince my words even one little bit. I told her it wasn't a question of whether she could or couldn't get over it, but whether or not she *wanted* to get over it, and it could be she was quite enjoying that little streak of vengeance she seemed unwilling to part with; whether or not he was the right one for her was not really important—it was the marriage relationship she was already *in* that was important!

I'd say I scored about zero. When I hung up, I was angry. Not at her—she's such a babe in Christ, I couldn't help thinking that her reactions were more than natural. But *I* was taking the full responsibility that she hadn't responded with a supernatural reaction. Momentarily, I'd forgotten that I work in cooperation *with* God, not separately and apart *from* Him. And so, I took on a burden that was too heavy for me to carry. I knew the words I'd spoken were words of truth. But the decision was wholly hers, and separate from me. I could not coerce her into making a proper decision. That had to be God's work, not mine.

Well, when Jamie made his profound statement I realized that I was trying to play God again and was back to some of my old tricks. With my arms around my boys, I confessed to God (and to them) that I had really pulled a "blooper" and that we needed a fresh start.

But when I prayed, I also put this young couple back into God's hands where they belonged. We'd been speaking the truth to them, telling them what they needed to do, Gene working with the sorrowful, deeply repentant husband and I with the distraught, unforgiving young wife. But now, we could only pray and be available if they wanted us. Sometimes, staying out of the way is the hardest part of counseling.

Well, this morning I had quite an experience. I was thinking about this pathetic wife, realizing that I had no idea what kind of pain this whole thing was causing her. But then I remembered something, a time several years ago when Gene and I were on one of the trips he'd won. Part of the trip was a dinner at some luxurious restaurant where you are squeezed into close proximity so that everyone in the tour can be seated. It so happened that an attractive, alluring tour-guide was seated beside my husband. I didn't mind that so much, but the fact that he turned toward her, with his back to me, for the duration of the meal was almost unbearable! It had been years since I'd had to bear such emotional hurt. Of course later he asked my forgiveness and said he had no idea it was hurting me so. But why should that same emotional hurt begin to move in and engulf me today? Why should that even pop into my memory? I was feeling the same hurt *all over again!* I tried rebuking Satan and then went on praising God, but the mood just wouldn't lift!

I finally decided God was trying to show me something. First this was the only feeling I'd ever had that would even give me some small notion of what this young wife was going through. I think God allowed me to have this memory recalled so that I might have more compassion for her. I had perhaps tended to be impatient with her last night on the phone.

But there was something nagging at me still, something that was trying to come through, something that was having a battle. And then, like a million-watt bulb popping, I realized what had happened.

It was possible for me to feel hurt from that episode because I had not entirely yielded my "right" to my husband's attention at that particular time! In these past many months, I have experienced the joy of "giving-living," where you give up all rights to your loved ones, all rights to their attention, all rights to their affection; and then when God gives you these rights back again, you can thank Him and praise Him for these things as "privileges," not demanded "rights"!

I made the beautiful discovery that you can go back to a given point in time, give up your "right" to your husband, even though the episode has passed, and be freed from the emotional ache you'd suffered from grasping onto one of your so-called rights!

In that moment that I gave up my right to my precious husband for a time in the past, I experienced a complete release from the ache! Satan was defeated, and Christ reigned supreme! For the Word tells us that "you shall know the truth and the truth shall make you free." Hallelujah!

34

It isn't very poetic trying to get a piece of bacon out of a package that's sealed as though it were going into a time capsule. It won't exactly send spiritual goosebumps down your spine when I tell you that Mark's turtle will definitely have emphysema if he doesn't change the water tonight. It won't draw you any closer to the Lord to know that something is wrong with our water system, and when the upstairs stool is flushed the whole house rattles, china jingles, and pipes clang so badly that even the bells in the telephone start ringing—so much so, that Larry opened his bedroom door and quietly intoned, "Would someone please answer the *plumbing!*"

No, it won't do a whole lot for you, but it will warm your heart and make you realize that "home" here is "home" just like it is at your house.

I sometimes think we picture the early Christians as so busy watching miracles and doing great deeds that they didn't have anything but spiritual "happenings" all the time. Sometimes we lose sight of the fact that they were people with problems and dispositions just like ours. We think they went around healing everybody; yet we read that Paul told Timothy to take wine because of a stomach problem. We read that Paul and Peter had a bit of a personality problem (which gives me great encouragement when I fail to respond as lovingly as I should to others). We find that Paul had one awful time with Alexander the silversmith, and didn't mind taking some pains to warn others that Alexander was his enemy.

Poor Euodias and Syntyche! Quite frankly, I think their names were enough to make them disagreeable. But they had one awful time hanging in there in real fellowship.

And poor Mark! Known as one of the early streakers, he dashed off into oblivion without his clothes in one of his weaker moments, and I'd say that the apostle Paul had a bit of a time forgiving him for his weakness.

We have Rahab, the loose woman who lied, yet God counts it to her for righteousness.

We have Hosea being commanded by God to marry a harlot.

We have a word of greeting extended to "Nymphas and the congregation who meet in *her* house" (Phillips, Amplified). What? A woman in charge of a house church?

So what do we find? We find everyday, normal people in charge of being responsible for the kingdom of God, by His Spirit. We have the Spirit giving life, not the letter of the law. We have flesh and blood people—the Davids whose hearts are right with God even though their sins are obnoxious in the nostrils of a holy God.

We have Abraham who is counted as a friend of God, in spite of his weakness and fears. We have imperfect people pebbled throughout the Scripture who have not been painted as frilly, or pedestal-elevated. They are just people—redeemed people. Imperfect people who have embraced a perfect Christ. People with hurts, with problems, with children. People who started at a certain place in time and history to become like the Christ they embraced. People who finally learned that the secret was in allowing Christ to live His life through them instead of striving to be godlike apart from His Spirit.

And so, what do we have here in this year of our Lord? Mothers who taxi aloof children from place to place, yet, the Spirit of God gives comfort to them and says this is part of the overall picture. It gives meaning to the comments that have unintentional hurts behind them like Laurie's "Mother, don't touch me . . . there are people watching" as you barely touch her hand to pull her a bit closer to shout above the basketball roar. Then she leaps into another cheer-leading routine and you sit there helplessly realizing that she wants a see-no-mother, hear-no-mother, speak-no-mother driver.

131

He is the same God of comfort who cushions the blows for us mothers as He cushioned the blows for our mothers when he did the same unintentional kind of hurting things to them. He is the same God of comfort who understood the aching heart of a Hannah, and the hurt that you endure from those you love the most.

Yes, He is the same God and we are the same kind of flesh and blood people He has been dealing with since Adam and Eve.

35

Before I started this book, I was toying with the idea of writing a book called *Welcome to a Warehouse*. It would contain events— some miraculous, some merely astounding—that happened to those of us who attend Zion Chapel at our beloved warehouse. But I'd no more than gotten through the first chapter when the fire marshal informed us that since we were squeezing people in until they were almost hanging out of the windows (much like Eutychus of old), we would have to make some improvements to meet the safety requirements before we could continue with our meetings. However, when we found out what the price of improvements would be, we started looking for another suitable place to meet. (So many people have said, "Why don't you build a church?" This is our answer: Why should we? There are many available places and who wants to get all tied up in knots with a building program? I'm happy to say that the money that comes flowing into Zion goes right out again for the Lord's work and for the care of people in need. Praise God!)

But because I had such a good time with chapter 1, and as it *does* describe our meetings, I think I'll slip it in here. Also, since we've now been out of the warehouse for over a year, it gave me some tender feelings of nostalgia just to read over what I'd written. So bear with me and let the other members of Zion get a little teary-eyed over past experiences.

Christ made His first entrance into our lives in a manger. There were no luxurious surroundings. Only the lowing of the animals, and the soft humming of the young mother who had borne Him, just a few hours before. I doubt if the aromas of that first dwelling place were pleasant. Earthy, pungent, but probably not pleasant. But this was His choice, His way of coming to us; and where Jesus is, all things seem right.

Perhaps this is why He is so willing to be a part of His people no matter where they meet. His Word to us is simply, "Where two or three are gathered together in my name, there am I in the midst of them." That's why people are gathering in barns, in warehouses, in little groups over the lunch period in the cafeteria, in coffee houses, anywhere because the hunger for reality is there, not for showiness and "atmosphere."

But here, come with us. Slip right into the front seat of the car with us as we make our way across town, past impressive edifices that are tolling the Sunday school hour as we wend our way through the traffic, then out into the country past some farm lands and finally to our beloved warehouse. Before long you will catch some of the anticipation we are feeling, but you won't really feel it until we wade through some of the chatter in the back seat of the car.

From Laurie, our teen-ager, you'll hear, "Mom, tell dad to hurry" (as though he couldn't hear her himself). "We're going to be late! Why do we always have to be late?"

My answer comes back, "Honey, when the Lord gets us all synchronized no doubt we will be on time. Until then, we will have to pray more fervently against a demon that breaks shoestrings, loses sox, spills milk, tears buttons off, and makes people grumpy! Plus, we could use a little more organization on Saturday night. But that takes discipline, and discipline being our weak point . . ."

With this lengthy explanation came two sharp salutes from Mark and Jamie, who then proceed to stick their tongues out at Laurie the moment our back is turned, . . . and then the word from Gene that "we are almost there."

Oh, look! It's coming into sight now. Well, after all, I told you it was a warehouse! But you won't mind at all when you get inside.

The walls are freshly painted a cozy cream color that we like to refer to as "Hallelujah yellow," and there are even curtains. You'll like it, honest. (All the while I'm wondering if you might leap out of the car when we stop for the red light. After *all*, it beats a store-front!)

And in a way you are right. No bells. No shrubbery. No stained-glass windows. No organ. No choir. No robes. No committee meetings, ever. (But no choir practice, either!)

Now, come along. Don't back out now. Let me tell you what the professor said when he gave a testimony one night. "The closer I came to those white wooden stairs, the heavier my legs got. I said, 'Lord, You don't really mean I'm supposed to worship here? That there is anything worthwhile in there for me?' " And somewhat like Nathanael of old, he muttered, "Can any good thing come out of a warehouse?" He continued, "But the closer I came to that singing, and when I saw the joy on the faces of His people, I knew I'd come to the right place, and my feet took wings. The heaviness was gone from my legs—and also from my heart!"

But here, just before we go inside, take a look at this sign out front, see? CABINET SHOP. (The other side of the building was rented out to cabinetmakers.) You see, during the week much planing and chipping and cutting are done on these premises. But it doesn't even begin to compare with the planing and chipping that is done through the week by the Carpenter who manages the *other* side of the warehouse!

You'll notice that the grass is well taken care of. When we first saw the warehouse, Jody stood out here in the grass and exclaimed, "You're going to call this Zion Chapel? This place looks more like a fortress. Why don't you paint in huge letters "A mighty fortress is our God!"

But you are looking a little uneasy. Let's go inside. And, as you make your way up those white wooden steps something happens. As you open the door, you are greeted by a presence. A presence that gently, magnetically draws you to the far end where you hear music—sweet, ethereal, almost unreal—coming from the lips of blood-washed sinners who've been set free.

Many times people have said, "No choir? Why not, for heaven's sake?" and I reply, "That's why—for heaven's sake.

135

We are in a continual choir practice for the time when we will be one great choir there in eternity. There will be no solos in heaven, you know.''

Now, to the right here we have the furnace room, and to the left we have the nurs—bless you, you're not even listening to me, are you? Well, then. Let's go on in. I can see by the hunger on your face that the music and love you feel are drawing you to get closer, just as those hands of love drew me only a few short years ago.

But wait! Just before we go into the main room, please do something. Close your eyes for a moment. Doesn't it take you back in time? Back to the time when the saints met in caverns and caves and catacombs because of the growing opposition? Can't you see them in your mind's eye? Peter, Paul, perhaps Lydia, all kneeling at individual rocks, with flickering dim candles hanging about. The soft, quiet praise of personal hearts turned upward toward a personal God, their Father and Maker.

Oh, please, please. Don't ruin this hallowed moment with some sterile comment about seeking Him by faith and not by feeling. Our God is a God of feeling as He is a God of love! Can there be a more strongly felt emotion?

Oh, see? That sweet presence of Jesus is now bearing witness to your Spirit that all this is of Him! I can tell by the tears swimming in your eyes and the radiance on your face.

And see what a motley crowd is gathered here. You'll see the rich, the poor, the handicapped, the intellectuals, the lovely, the unlovable, all making harmony together because they are all one in the Spirit. Isn't that what it's all about? Didn't He pray ''that they all might be one, even as we are one''?

And softly, so softly, we slip into nearby seats and close our eyes. Raising our faces upward, we, too, bask in His love and warmth and become a part of this worshiping fellowship that He has raised up; and we become a part of the Body of Christ that meets in His warehouse, to His glory and honor.

Amen.

36

Recently I received this letter from a pastor's wife in a small rural community.

After introducing herself and expressing affectionate feelings for me (for which I am most grateful), she continued with the following:

I'd like to ask you about one statement in your book *If You See Lennie* that I have struggled with. Perhaps you can explain how you came to your position on it.

It was in letter 42 (p. 209). You were telling about visiting friends on Sunday night. You said, "Two services on Sunday can be exhausting (and her added footnote was 'you're right!') so we don't always go." Then a bit farther down you talked about the days when you thought 'if you really love the Lord you will be in church every time the doors are open.'

As you have probably guessed, I am the wife of a pastor of a small, struggling church in a pioneer area. And believe me—I really am not being ugly! I just want you to know. I realize there are times when we just can't be there, and everyone can't support all the organizations for every group in the church. But the times of worship together are so few, and we need each other's fellowship so much, I always think, Why do they assume the pastor and his family should *always* be there but the members have different "directions."

I guess a little selfishness creeps in there; I'm sorry. I truly love my Savior and want to do His will. And thank you again for writing the book. It lifted my heart and gave me a tremendous blessing.

Now, let me add another line from another letter. This reader said, "Being a preacher's wife, I'm often involved in church work that is unnecessary."

To me, the first letter states a problem, and the second letter states a fact. (And they may be one and the same!)

And so, feeling very much like a spiritual Ann Landers, let me hereby promptly get into more hot water by sharing with you my position.

Dear readers:

Having entered into His Sabbath rest, having nestled very comfortably into His loving arms, and being most cozy from this vantage point of looking down on the circumstances rather than focusing on them at eye level, I would like to state my full heart on this matter. I will not necessarily win friends and influence pastors, but you can be sure I will catch the ear of every tired saint who is anywhere in the vicinity!

Somehow, I feel as though we have made more of "forsaking not the assembling of ourselves together" than we should have. According to my dictionary, to forsake is to abandon or give up.

Now as I see it, missing an occasional meeting does not necessarily mean you are abandoning all meetings. And yet, as two or three of us meet over coffee, we are having "church." Take last night, for instance. Two ladies whom I'd never met called me from our store. The one who called said, "We've just discovered you are no longer meeting in the warehouse. Could you tell me where the meeting is?"

I responded, "We are no longer meeting in the warehouse, and we are also no longer meeting on Thursday nights. It's been changed to Wednesday nights."

A disappointed moan came from the other end of the conversation. "We had so hoped to find some fellowship! We are starving to talk with someone about the Lord. Do you know where there are *any* meetings tonight?''

I thought as hard as I could, and the words of Frank Gonzales came back to me. He always said, ''Go where the action is. And if there isn't any, start some!''

So I heard these words coming out of my mouth: ''I can't think of any meetings at all, but if you'd like to come over we can have a meeting of our own!''

And so, about half an hour later two perfect strangers marched into my house, and we fellowshiped at the feet of Jesus, worshiped Him, bared our hearts with one another, and talked freely about some very intimate problems they were having in their marriage. And when they left, I knew in my heart that we had all been cheered and refreshed—which should always be the case when we have been cleansed by His blood as we fellowship together.

You see, our hearts had burned as we talked about Him. We were warmed by His love as we prayed and looked to Him to be the solution to the problems they were presenting. In essence, we had had ''church.'' And it had all been arranged by the Holy Spirit! (I tell you, meetings that are arranged by the Holy Spirit are the very best!)

However, last Sunday we didn't go to *any* surlvices! (Do you still love us? Oh, I hope so!) The reason we didn't go to church is because my husband was sensitive enough to the Holy Spirit to see the tears trickling down my face as I was trying to make myself get the ball rolling to put forth that tremendous Sunday morning effort that is necessary to get us all ready on time.

He commented, ''You're exhausted, aren't you.'' It wasn't a question, it was an observation. I nodded, and cried like a baby. I was ashamed that it should be the Lord's day and my flesh should be so weak.

He sat down beside me on the bed. ''Char, I'm tired too. Somewhere, somehow along the way we have to have a 'day of rest and gladness.' I'm declaring one for us today.'' And it was done. I was too tired to worry about those who might not understand, as well as those few who might point a finger in judgment.

And as I was resting, greatly relieved that I was not going to have to push my tired body into the rigors that have to be endured to get us to church, I couldn't help thinking that most pastors and elders set aside a "family" day—a day when the rest of the congregation is notified that they are to let their problems wait for a more convenient time so that the leaders can have the prescribed day of rest that is needed for body rejuvenation. I couldn't help thinking of my poor husband, whose business required that he work a full six days a week, and often long hours into the night while driving long distances or staying up late with dealers, and so on. Then, immediately he's thrust into a heavy Sunday morning meeting schedule, into quick family visitings, never time for a nap, with no time to be a family if we go off to a Sunday night meeting, as he has to hit the road again the next day, or soon after!

Dear readers, love us in spite of our weakness. Love us even if we can't fit into the mold Christendom has made for us. Don't point a finger at the ones who don't come to every meeting, because God alone knows why they weren't there. And as He is the only one who knows the condition of every heart, let Him be the judge of the situation. Pray for them. And always bear in mind that attendance at meetings has never been a criterion for sainthood; rather, it's the condition of the heart.

You see, I have had to learn all of my lessons the hard way. I remember going off to Sunday evening meetings alone when I was still a part of the institutional church because Gene just wasn't all that interested in the things of God at that time. And there I would sit, trying not to feel homesick and guilt-ridden because my little family was home without me. So, wanting to combat these uncomfortable feelings, I would then try staying home with my family, only to find myself immersed in guilt again because I'd somehow picked up this notion that "those who really love the Lord will be there every time the door is open."

I was never freed from this until I began to see that my real ministry before the Lord was to "submit and adapt" to the husband God had given me.

You see, to me, loving Christ properly is allowing Him to reign in my innermost being, allowing Him to be the "hidden man of the heart." And loving Him properly means having my priorities straightened out.

Before, my priorities were lined up like this:

140

Christ

Church

Children

Husband

But they should have been:

Christ

Husband

Children

Church

And loving Him properly means having proper attitudes. In fact, I think this whole thing of Christian living has more to do with attitudes and motives than with anything else. I don't believe the Lord is nearly as interested in the final task that is finished, as He is in the *attitude* in which the task was performed and the *motive* that inspired you doing the task. "Whatsoever thy hand findest to do, do it *heartily* as unto the Lord." In other words, do it with a willing heart, not begrudgingly.

There are other misunderstandings that run rampant in the Body of Christ. I remember being put terribly under condemnation by this comment: "When you are not in your place in the meeting, you may have stopped the Body from hearing a special prophecy or message in tongues just because you were not there." (Do you see what a bondage this could become? One could soon think he was indispensable!) I heard someone using Thomas as an example. They said, "He missed a blessing because he wasn't there when Jesus showed up." And this is true. But if you read on a bit farther, Jesus showed up a second time just so Thomas *could* have a blessing! And God, who upbraideth not, never chided him about not being at the previous meeting!

And so, to the pastor's wife in the rural area, all my love. And to the pastor's wife who is involved in unnecessary church work, I give all my love. To those who feel that it is wrong to miss any meetings, we give our love. To those who will take unfair advantage of what I've said here (stand fast in the liberty wherein Christ hath made you free—only use not liberty for an occasion to the flesh), may God have mercy on you, and we give you our love. "And now abideth faith, hope, and charity (love), and *the greatest* of these is charity (*love*)" (italics mine).

37

If you read *If You See Lennie,* you'll recall an incident in letter 38 about a young boy who had stolen some pretty hefty merchandise from our store.

I am most happy to relate to you that he has made full resititution. I wish I could report to you the exact feelings that we all shared as he came in here with the last part of the payment, but my abilities as a writer fail at this point. Some things are just impossible to record.

We all rejoiced in God's faithfulness as Frank began to tell us of some of the unique ways God provided the means for him to make restitution.

You see, he'd stolen from other places as well as ours. The amount he had to pay back was $4,500, all totaled; but God had enabled him to do it in the space of eighteen months! He said that although he and his wife had had to say "no" to any luxuries, they had never gone without anything they truly needed. The discipline of this had caused him to grow and mature in the Lord in many other ways, besides. His little wife looked at him with real admiration because she knew this was a sacrifice for him as well as for herself, but the feeling of satisfaction in knowing that they had done what pleased God was so great it far surpassed any loss they could have experienced.

He said that often God would just move on the hearts of people to give money to him. (I'm not even sure that too many knew he was making restitution until, somehow, word leaked out just toward the end before restitution had been completed.)

God is really so good. Oh, how I hope you've noticed!

38

The most precious thoughts I have had, and the sweetest things the Spirit has spoken to me will never be known because the Spirit of God flits them into my consciousness; and by the time I've stirred myself from my bed or have flown from the dishwater to put them down on paper, they are gone. Still, they remain a part of my consciousness, and by faith I believe that the Spirit of God will bring them back to me whenever He needs them for His own use.

If there is any one thing that is frustrating about being a woman, it is the need to repress the impulse to shout from the housetops what He tells me in secret. Women preachers are not exactly sought after, yet God has placed His Spirit here within this womanly frame of mine, and I cannot deny the deep stirrings of grace He gives to me—stirrings that are meant to be shared with you, the Body of Christ. Does not the Word say that He will pour out His Spirit upon his menservants *and* His handmaidens? I can't help but feel that that outpouring was for more than just establishing a godly atmosphere in the home, important as that is.

But with the outpouring of His Spirit, many things are attendant. First, a desire to tell the whole world and second, a desire to "know God" as you have never known anyone before. And a natural reaction to this is to talk of Him, every waking moment, every breath, with every movement you make, constantly referring to this wonderful Jesus. Yet, women are stopped short so often by disapproving looks, by a living by "the letter of the law" which so often kills the Spirit. For where the Spirit of the Lord is, there is liberty.

Sometimes, I feel almost apologetic when I come before the Lord. Almost, as if I have to say, "Sir, I am here before You with a deep, burning desire to tell the world about You, of Your faithfulness to me, But did You make a mistake, Sir? I mean, I'm a woman. Shouldn't You have given these burning desires to someone else—a man, perhaps, Sir?" But then, I quickly come to my senses and realize that He has made no mistake, that He knew exactly what He was doing, and that the burning desires within me were inspired by the very Spirit of God himself. So I pull out all the stops, let myself go, and praise Him for making me just the way He wanted me.

All this has come about because of a singing heart. Sometimes, there is just no way to contain the joy I feel within, and I have to prattle it all out on the typewriter and pray that you, my readers, my dear, devoted, seeing-no-fault-in-me readers will somehow be blessed by what I have written.

I just read in the Amplified Bible Psalm 18:19 and 20 that "he brought me forth also into a large place; he was delivering me, because he was pleased with me and delighted in me. The Lord rewarded me according to my righteousness . . . with him, according to the cleanness of my hands has he recompensed me." And it all caused such a wave of gratitude to flood over me, I just had to share it with you.

Truly, I have been brought into a large place. No more am I being twisted and squeezed and dominated by my emotions. But I have emerged into a large place, one of right and proper attitudes, a place where I am being dominated by *His Spirit,* not by immature attitudes that gripped and plagued me and caused me to be held back from freedom, from soaring and expanding! I have elbow room here. I have an abundance of energy, for it is not being drained and wasted emotionally in thinking only of my own needs, my "rights." I can "leap over walls" that have grown up between myself and others because of my God (v. 29).

And in this "large place" I realize that it isn't how many meetings I go to, how much I clap my hands or shout, how much I do for the Body of Christ, but what really matters to my God is that which is done in secret! The important things are those that are screened from the prying, misunderstanding eyes of men: the life that is "hidden with Christ," the motives, the attitudes; these are what really matter, because they constitute my "righteousness." (In brackets in the Amplified Bible it says, "my conscious integrity and sincerity with him.")

Integrity is defined as "honesty-sincerity." But it must be honesty in the inmost parts—down deep, where only God can see. Yes, the Bible clearly states that my heart is deceitful and desperately wicked.

But there, in the midst of that deceitful heart, holding full sway is the very Spirit of God himself. You know, it is no marvel to me that He submitted to being born in a manger, a place of filth and refuse. But the wonder is that He would choose to reign in the filth and degradation of the human heart surrounded by the wickedness that every human heart is capable of!

39

Wow! Such feelings stirring within. How do I sort them out? How do I put them into intelligible sentences for you? By "bringing into captivity every thought to the obedience of Christ." And I have a peculiar way of doing that. When a disturbing thought enters, I pick it up as though it was a piece of lettuce, and I hand it to Christ as though I was a small raccoon that it might be rinsed off and cleansed by Him. Crazy, you say? A bit. But it works and I think it is Scriptural, as we are told to "try every spirit whether they be of God." Now, if you think I've scrambled that one up a bit, look in the Amplified Bible and see if it doesn't say in Proverbs 16:2, "All the ways of a man are pure in his own eyes, but the Lord weighs the spirits—*the thoughts and intents of the heart.*"

And so, since spirits gain entrance through the mind, through the thought life, I think it is true that we must examine them closely with the Lord.

But maybe the Spirit of God can draw all this out better if I use an experience I've just recently had.

In the midst of a discussion, someone was giving out the importance of the cross, the need we have to "die" as a kernel of wheat that has fallen into the ground, that this is where it all is, in "death." Now, before I lose half my readers, I'd like to say, "Amen. This is where it is." But there is more that needs to be said than just this. Would not this be a message of gloom and despair to a new Christian? And I knew there were some there who were very weak in the faith; so I proceeded to say what I felt was stirring inside of me, when someone said, "Well, you can understand these things because you've experienced this death and you already know that you are nothing. Haven't you, Char?" (It was more of a declaration than a question.)

I grimaced. How I wished I could say to them that I was "utterly dead" to self, but what a liar I would have made of myself. Instead, I said, "Hold it. We are acting as though this were a one-time commitment, a once and for all thing. People, I don't believe that that is the way it is. I believe it is a process. Otherwise, why would the Lord tell us to 'take up our cross and die daily'?

"When they nailed Christ on the cross, the act was called 'crucifixion,' but the 'dying' was a process. If it took the Son of God six hours to die, and if one day is as a thousand with Him, does it not stand to reason that it will take us a whole lifetime to die to this "self"—this core of self that will remain with us until we go to be with the Lord? Is this not the reason for our need of continual repentance? Because there is within us a root, a blight, that we must live with until we see His face?

"Yet, we can praise God because He exchanged this core of sin within us for the righteousness (in other words, the 'right ways') of His dear Son, Jesus. And so, though that sinful nature remains with us, we can die to it and not let it hold full sway in our lives by coming against those natural inclinations that have their root in the self life. When we come against those natural inclinations, we are dying to self and manifesting the resurrection life that He has given us.

"But even though I say I have died (although it is an established fact in history that when God looks at me He sees me perfect in His Son Jesus because *Jesus died in my place*), yet I have not *experientially* died entirely to self. Nevertheless, I have learned in many instances the value of saying no to self, thus allowing His life to flow through me and into the particular situation. Yet there have been so many times when I have allowed my *own* need to loom up as more important than the need of the other person, and I realize in retrospect that I was as blatantly alive to 'self' as I had been previous to my conversion experience."

Then I'm afraid I startled them by saying, "And as for my being nothing, hey, I've got *news* for you. I'm *something*! I'm the only

147

person running around just exactly like me. I am absolutely unique! There isn't another quite like me in all the universe, or down through the ages. I'm the only one exactly like 'me' who will ever be!''

I saw some there who were a bit appalled at such a bold statement, so I added, ''Now realize, I know there is no good thing in my flesh, in this sin nature of mine that likes to rear its ugly head. But how can I love my neighbor as myself if I don't like the 'me' that God created? How can I be comfortable with others if I am not comfortable with myself? Darlings, it's taken me too many years to come this far, too many bumps. Don't try and take it from me now. Don't misunderstand what I'm saying. I am grateful to my God because it is His mighty power stirring in me that has made me become all the things I have ever wanted to be.

No, dear ones, if I think of myself as 'nothing' then I must think of my neighbor also as 'nothing' if I am to love him as myself. But I think of him as someone with great worth because he was created in the image of God. My neighbor is valuable to God in the same way that I am valuable—because of my worth as a human being.''

And then we laughed because I was so exuberant that I was flinging my arms and hands all over trying to express myself. I told them it was most frustrating when I went to put these things down on paper, as it's impossible to type and fling your arms about at the same time.

40

I am staring here at a heap of typewritten pages that is to eventually become this book you are reading. Somehow, I must put it all together so that it flows with at least a measure of continuity. Me, the scatterbrained, typically helpless female, facing an assignment like that! It would seem far more reasonable if the Lord had given this task to some of these well-organized, detail-loving people with whom I've been acquainted. But no, His ways are past finding out and His thoughts are not our thoughts. He loves doing the impossible and using the most unlikely.

And if getting all this into graceful, flowing book form seems like a problem, just try *ending* a book! How do you end something that keeps going on? Eternal life, I mean. And that's what I've prayed my words have been to you—eternal life-giving words, hopefully fresh and pure.

But I think God gave me an inkling yesterday, as to how the book should be ended. I was about to go to the basement and sort the clothes when it occurred to me that that would be a great time to listen to a tape. Then I remembered that Alice had given me a tape of her testimony, and I could't think of better company while I was working. So I slipped the tape into place and quietly listened to Alice's testimony while I was sorting clothes heartily, as "unto the Lord."

I had asked Alice some months ago if she minded if I put her testimony into this book. She said no, she didn't mind. However, we had a hard time getting together to put some of the facts

149

straight.

Finally, two days ago, she shyly slipped the tape into my hands and said, "Char, I really kind of bared my heart. But you pick and choose, and use what you feel should be shared." And all the highbrowish bluestocking within me ceremoniously held up its head and solemnly said, "Yes, dear, just the facts. I'll put it all together nicely."

And I will humbly tell you that after I'd heard the first three sentences I knew this was from the Lord and I would be committing a sacrilege if I were even to change one "jot or tittle."

I have Alice's permission to share her tape in its entirety, word for word, tear for tear.

Char, I came from a home that was full of love. I had a good childhood. We were quite poor but there was always love, and I often saw my daddy affectionate to my mother. God bless her, she's a good woman and I love her dearly. She always did what she thought was right and I thank her for this. Anyway, she told me that you had to grow up and be a good girl and not do anything wrong because guys just didn't marry girls that were easy. So I had very few dates, had lots of complexes about being homely, and besides the war was on so there weren't too many guys around when I was at the dating age.

But when I met that tall blond guy with the rosy cheeks and cute smile, I really fell and I fell hard. He was home on furlough and was kind of an innocent kid. He really treated me like a queen. Well, he went back to base and it wasn't long until I had an engagement ring. I really didn't know Bob that well, but I thought he was pretty great the little time I was with him which I think amounted to about two weeks.

He was over in Panama for a year. During that time I was asked out on dates occasionally, the first time in all the years, I guess, but I refused them. I was going to save myself for him. And consequently, I missed a lot of good times, I guess; but anyway I waited for him and he finally came home. Being young and in love, all I could think about was getting married. He said, "Sure, we'll get married, we'll get married."

Finally I said something about the date and we decided we'd get married the first of May. But my mom said, "Oh, no, you must have a church wedding and you've got to do it all proper and send out invitations," and the whole bit. That was fine, I guess, but in our childish, selfish way, we begrudged my mother that little thrill of having that wedding. So I went to bed with Bob and I became pregnant.

Well, it seemed like everything was great and Bob didn't appear to regret it. But year after year I tortured myself with the idea that because I let him touch me before marriage I had committed adultery and I was in sin. I privately asked God's forgiveness, but I felt He never forgave me. That shows you how stupid I was in the Word. Every time Bob and I had a fight or anything would go wrong I'd keep thinking that he didn't love me because I was easy and he *had* to marry me. I spent a good many years in anguish over this.

Time went on and one child arrived after another, and about four years after we were married I found out Bob was going blind. It didn't matter to me because I loved him so much. I was just young enough to believe I could do anything, so we tried to build a home. In the middle of the project one of our children got sick and I had to quit my work. Bob had to go to Ann Arbor and have surgery and experimental work on his eyes because he was going slowly blind mainly from cataracts, but they thought it was *retinitis pigmentosa* that was deteriorating his eyes.

Anyway, in the process of all our problems we were going to lose the home that Bob and I had been building. To Bob it was kind of like a status symbol to have that home. He was handicapped and everybody knew he was and he wanted to prove himself to be a man. He held a job down—in fact, sometimes two—and he was a loving father and played with the kids and wanted everything for them, and I loved him for it.

But, you know, after that house, the disappointment of it and all, we'd turned from God, and about the same time we dropped our church. The kids decided they didn't like Sunday school, and it was easier to sleep on Sunday mornings. We worked split shifts, sometimes nights. And so, somehow or other we got away from church.

Well, time passed and it seemed like we kept getting on each other's nerves continually. Some place back in those years I found out that he hadn't been faithful to me while we were engaged. He had a girl in Panama and that gnawed and gnawed at me and I should have let it drop, but Christ wasn't in my heart. I just couldn't seem to capture what I've found now.

Anyway, the years passed and I started being the dominating mother. I was frustrated because I wanted so much for my children to be honest, law-abiding citizens, a credit to society—and everything that goes with that. I demanded the house must be clean (you can be poor, but clean—you know, all the attributes a woman feels should be right.)

But do you know, I forgot to *love*! I'm not talking about kissing and hugging because I think I did that. But when I spoke, I spoke with authority instead of love, and I didn't let God rule the house. And I didn't let my husband be the leader; I let Alice be the domineering force with all her little subjects under her, and I *know* I did this. I really didn't realize I was doing it until this terrible tragedy happened.

Bob had had this trouble with his eyes, but he worked daily and always had respect and admiration from everybody around him because he could handle a job. But one day they came up with a new cleaning solution that he was allergic to, and it caused horrible blisters on his eyes. He started doctoring, but all of a sudden the doctor announced, "He's got to quit work." And we were thousands of dollars in debt! Also, by that time we had two kids in college. We'd had a couple of big weddings we'd gone into debt for, and we'd bought new furniture and had a car to pay for—oh, so many things, besides illnesses. I'd had cancer, and although God had spared my life, there was plenty of debt from this staring us in the face.

And so, Bob had to quit work. And never in the world did I think I'd have to go through what I did! I knew I would have to go through traumas with Bob, but somehow he had to face the future, still a young man and yet so old in so many ways. Retired at forty-seven, his life, to him, was about over.

And my heart went out to him. Yet at the same time I was bitter because my son had gotten himself into a scrape and joined the

152

army just to stay out of jail. And I was bitter to Bob because he didn't speak up and make the boy mark the old chalkline that I had always set for him. So Robbie, our youngest, went into the service. And here were Bob and I, just the two of us. And I thought, "It's not so bad. Somehow we'll manage these debts. Bob loves to cook and putter in the yard and I can work during the day and come home to a nice cooked meal. Then it won't take long for us to clean up the house and we can go fishing and traveling when things get all right—his pension was fairly decent. We could live comfortably on what I made. I had the whole future planned, and nothing could hurt us anymore. God had spared me from cancer! And He spared Bob's eyes enough so he could get around, bait his hook, saw his boards, and do little things in the garden.

But Char, Bob found someone else, a young girl who had had a hard life. And he wanted her, oh, he wanted her more than anything in the world. (I tried to believe he didn't really want her, that he just wanted a new lease on life, something to make him feel younger again.) And so he asked for a divorce. My heart was broken, I had already had *so* many heartaches. He went to his dad, but he turned him away. However, our daughter, Kathy, said, "Come live with me." Kathy told me how I'd been cross and irritable and had never shown anybody love. I was hurt so badly! Everything that I stood for was just shot to the wind. Being good and decent wasn't anything anymore. Our children stood up for him for having an affair with a young girl.

I begged the girl, I talked with her and told her, "You *can't* do this, you can't take this man I spent my life with. You can't take him now that everything's just going to work out." But it was too late, Char. He left me. She'd shown him kindness and he had no more feeling for me.

Char, I lost my mind. I went crazy. I was living on sleeping pills to get to sleep at night and tranquilizers in the day. I couldn't live without him. He was as much a part of me as my own heart was. After several weeks, I called my doctor and said, "You have to help me." He put me in the hospital and I don't even remember what happened. I just know that they had me under sedation and after a few weeks they started sending me to Oak Lawn psychiatric center.

Oh, the story could go on forever because there's so much to remember. It hurts even now to remember all this. But I know one thing: in all these years I've been searching and not knowing what was missing from my life. My church, I felt, let me down and I kept searching for the right place, the right things. I didn't know what it was, but something was missing.

And then I met Edie. Edie invited me to your prayer meeting one Tuesday night and I thought, "Oh God, I can't face it. I can't go and be joyful and loving the Lord when I am so confused." (I know now that God was working, for even then He was pushing and prodding me, but I didn't want to come to Him. I wanted to suffer more, I guess.)

All the while I thought I'd forgiven Bob and thought I could get over him. And I came to your prayer meeting that night and sat down and talked about it, and I saw the joy in your faces and the happiness, and you talked so *boldly* about the Lord and the Holy Spirit and how He worked in your lives! Everywhere I looked there was such joy, and yet I was *so* miserable. And I wanted what you all had! I wanted to find the Lord in the way you had found Him. I wanted to know the Lord as my Savior, and I told you so. And that night you all came and laid your hands on me and prayed for me. And I remember a voice like from heaven saying, "Oh, Alice, get that *hate* out of your heart, get that *hate* out!" And something made me scream it out to you. And Char, you cast out that spirit of hate in the name of Jesus. And you told me to rebuke Satan, and I did. And it was just like something calmed my heart. There was no music, there wasn't any noise; there was just a calm, sweet peace that came over me. And from that day on, I truly couldn't hate.

I won't say that all of my problems disappeared overnight because they didn't. But the hate was gone, and every time I thought about what went on that night, a great new feeling came over me. I became bold to talk about the Lord. I wanted to read, I wanted to study, and I wanted to know more. It seems like everything I do now, I want to please the Lord. Oh, I slip and I fall and I get back up, but I still feel that the Lord is working in my life. My children have turned back to me, and they love me and respect me for what I've become. I know I've got to learn to love more; and

I've got to teach my children that you cannot *demand* love, you must *earn* it. And only through the Lord can I make them understand the real way toward a happy marriage or happy life of any kind. I know, too, that you've got to make the most of every day and do the best you can.

So Char, that's my story. I don't think my story has even really begun because God's got a new plan and I'm really anxious to know what it is. I think sometimes that's the hardest part—being patient until He shows you the way. But I do know one thing: I'm ready and willing to do anything God has planned, and I give my whole heart and soul to Him. Never again will I falter because now I know the truth. God bless you Char, Alice.